BLUEPRINT
Infant Geography Resource Bank

Sue Thomas

Stephen Scoffham

Stanley Thornes (Publishers) Ltd

Do you receive BLUEPRINTS NEWS?

Blueprints is an expanding series of practical teacher's ideas books and photocopiable resources for use in primary schools. Books are available for separate infant and junior age ranges for every core and foundation subject, as well as for an ever widening range of other primary teaching needs. These include **Blueprints Primary English** books and **Blueprints Resource Banks**. **Blueprints** are carefully structured around the demands of National Curriculum in England and Wales, but are used successfully by schools and teachers in Scotland, Northern Ireland and elsewhere.

Blueprints provide :
- *Total curriculum coverage*
- *Hundreds of practical ideas*
- *Books specifically for the age range you teach*
- *Flexible resources for the whole school or for individual teachers*
- *Excellent photocopiable sheets - ideal for assessment and children's work profiles*
- *Supreme value*

Books may be bought by credit card over the telephone and information obtained on **(0242) 228485.** Alternatively, photocopy and return this **FREEPOST** form to receive **Blueprints News**, our regular update on all new and existing titles. You may also like to add the name of a friend who would be interested in being on the mailing list.

Text © Sue Thomas and Stephen Scoffham 1994
Original line illustrations by Mark Dunn © ST(P) Ltd 1994

First published in 1994 by:
Stanley Thornes (Publishers) Ltd
Ellenborough House
Wellington Street
CHELTENHAM GL50 1YD
England

A catalogue record for this book is available from the British Library.

ISBN 0–7487–1731–5

Typeset by Tech-Set, Gateshead, Tyne & Wear.
Printed in Great Britain at The Bath Press, Avon

CONTENTS

INTRODUCTION

The **Blueprints** *Geography Resource Banks* have been devised to provide an encyclopaedic resource of photocopiable material for teachers of geography in primary schools. The *Infant Geography Resource Bank* provides material for 5–7 year olds, the *Junior Geography Resource Bank* for 7–11 year olds. The books can be used alongside all UK geography curricula and are designed, unlike conventional worksheets, to provide materials which can be used with great flexibility to meet individual classroom needs.

The Infant Geography Resource Bank

The book provides 107 photocopiable copymasters together with teacher's notes, topic index and a curriculum matrix linking the material to the National Curriculum for England, Wales and Northern Ireland, and the 5–14 Guidelines for Scotland.

The book is divided into nine sections, each of which covers an important geographical theme and often links directly with familiar infant-school topics. The sections are:

- Homes and settlements
- Different places
- Maps
- Making things
- People who help us
- Moving around
- Water in the environment
- Weather and climate
- Looking at the land.

The *Infant Geography Resource Bank* covers all appropriate aspects of geography for this age range. There is a careful balance of physical, human and environmental geography, as well as map work and geographical skills which are tested in context. Special attention has also been placed on the study of real places for infants, which satisfies the requirement for studies of different places and knowledge of the wider world in all the UK curricula. The localities chosen are: Wembury in Devon; Stevenage in Hertfordshire; and Chinon in France.

Using the copymasters

The copymasters provide a huge bank of picture information, maps, templates and source material which you can call upon as you wish. They can be used to:

- introduce geographical vocabulary
- practise map and atlas skills
- prompt discussion and research

- provide information about specific places
- make classroom wall displays
- assess geography skills and knowledge
- link geography into cross-curricular infant topics.

The children will want to colour many of the copymasters. They can also cut them up and use them in sequencing activities, individual booklets, class scrapbooks and games. If copymasters are to be reused, it may be an idea to stick them on to card and laminate them. For matching activities, where children have to place pictures and/or labels around the borders, it is a good idea to stick the copymasters on to large (A3 or A2) sheets of paper before distributing them among the class. Depending on the needs of your class, you may want to adapt the copymasters or turn them into workcards. This approach can help to provide for differentiation.

In order to make them as flexible as possible you will find that the copymasters themselves do not carry specific instructions for use. Instead you will find a range of concise suggestions in the teacher's notes on how to use each copymaster. The notes also identify cross-curricular links. History, art, maths, data handling, IT, science, technology, health and safety, English and environmental education have all been considered. Many of the activities draw widely on language skills. The 'Maps' section, for instance, contains maps based on stories and rhymes in order to make them appropriate to young children.

It is left to you to decide on the level of teacher involvement in each activity, as this will vary depending on the children's ages and abilities. Accordingly, activities may be carried out by the teacher, by the teacher working with the children or by the children working alone; the children may work individually, in pairs or in groups.

Using the copymasters in lesson planning

The topic index allows you to find all the copymasters which could be useful for a particular cross-curricular topic. For example, if you were teaching the children about 'Ourselves' you could select copymasters 1–10, 68–74, 91 and 95–6 from the sections on 'Homes and settlements', 'Making things', 'People who help us' and 'Weather and climate'.

There is also a matrix showing how the main themes in the book relate to the National Curriculum Orders for England, Wales, Scotland and Northern Ireland. This highlights the breadth and balance of the material and will help you to plan geography topics.

TOPIC INDEX

PRIMARY CURRICULUM COVERAGE FOR ENGLAND AND WALES, SCOTLAND AND NORTHERN IRELAND

○ Some coverage of requirements
● Nearly full coverage of requirements

National Curriculum England and Wales	Homes and settlements	Different places	Maps	Making things	People who help us	Moving around	Water in the environment	Weather and climate	Looking at the land
Skills	○	○	○	○	○		○	○	○
Places	○	●	○		●				
Physical geography							○	○	○
Human geography	○	○		○	○	○			
Environmental geography				●			○		
Scotland: National Guidelines for Environmental Studies 5–14 Understanding people and places									
Aspects of physical and built environment								●	○
Ways in which places have affected people and people have used and affected places	○	○			○			○	
Locations, linkages, networks						○			
Making and using maps		○	●		○				
Northern Ireland Curriculum Order (valid until 1996)									
AT1 Methods of geographical enquiry	○		○				○	○	○
AT2 Physical environments								○	○
AT3 Human environments	○	○		○	○	○			
AT4 Place and space	○	○	○						
AT5 Issues				○		○			○

HOMES AND SETTLEMENTS ▶

Copymaster 1 (A village in the countryside)
Cut out the word boxes and use them to label the picture.

Use the word boxes to start or add to a spelling book of geographical vocabulary.

Label and picture from
Copymaster 10 with child's
own drawing

Label from Copymaster 10
with child's own drawing

Book of geography vocabulary

Colour the picture using different colours for homes, shops etc. and make a colour key.

Make a postcard that shows an interesting view of the village: one that could be sold in the village shop (this could be adapted for role play). To practise recognition of geographical features, you could specify which features to include or give different groups separate lists of features. One list could include the school, shop and recreation field, for example, and a second list could include the farm, lane and animals. The children can use the back of the card to write a message about the village; if they include their home address they will practise their personal geographical knowledge. Children could then post the card home.

Copymaster 2 (A village by the sea)
Compare the village shown here with the other two in this section – record the similarities and differences.

Use this picture to talk about holidays by the sea. What would the children do here on holiday? Record their answers inside a large collage of a harbour or harbour wall.

Use the picture to discover how places are changed by the holiday trade. Mark down what is old and what is new (link with history and environmental education).

Use crayons or paints to show what happens here in a storm (link with art).

Cut out the word boxes to label the picture.

Copymaster 3 (A village in a mining valley)
Use with Copymasters 1 and 2 to make displays of different kinds of villages.

Sort the buildings into those used to live in and those used for work. Colour them differently.

Compare this village with your local area. How is it similar and how is it different?

Cut up the picture and make it into a jigsaw for the children.

Cut out the word boxes to label the picture.

Copymaster 4 (A market town)
Use the word boxes to label the picture.

Shuffle the cut-out word boxes. Ask each child to choose four and write about a visit to the town that incorporates these places. (If several copies of the copymaster are used, care is needed to ensure that two or more of the same places aren't chosen.)

Compare this scene with a town in your local area.

Use the picture as a basis for artwork, building up a busy street scene as a class or group activity.

Copymaster 5 (A town near London)
Use the picture to write a list of the things found in a town.

Colour all the places that are concerned with journeys.

Colour the picture to show the different areas of the town – commercial, housing and leisure.

Use the word boxes and symbols to label parts of the town.

Use the symbols on pictures and maps of your local area.

Copymaster 6 (A new town)
Use this copymaster with 'Different places – Stevenage' (Copymasters 16–18) to practise map skills, matching areas of the town.

Use each of the three headings to start a page about places in your local area that are similar or different.

Make sets of buildings, using these pictures to start with and adding more from magazines (link with data handling/IT).

Make a guide book for this town, the children adding a piece of descriptive writing to match each picture (link with English).

Copymaster 7 (A capital city – London)
Use the copymaster as a discussion picture to talk about the famous buildings of London and their uses.

Colour all the ways people make journeys in London.

Cut out the word boxes and use them to label the picture.

Split the class into groups and ask each group to paint and write about the different labels to make a class book.

Copymaster 8 (A modern city – Plymouth)
Use the pictures to discuss why Plymouth seems so new. (War damage meant the city needed almost total rebuilding.)

Compare the buildings with those in York on Copymaster 9.

Make large pictures of the boxes to create a set of postcards.

Write imaginary accounts of a visit to Plymouth (link with English).

Use this copymaster with 'Different places – Wembury' (Copymasters 11–15). Plymouth is the nearest city and Plymothians use Wembury as one of the nearest beaches. Make a page to show that people in Wembury shop and work in Plymouth. Discuss the difference between a village and a city or the fact that people from Plymouth go to Wembury for leisure.

Compare the buildings with those in your nearest city. The tourist information offices will send you leaflets that may be helpful.

Make a model of the sundial or use a shadow stick to try telling the time in the playground (link with science).

Copymaster 9 (An old city – York)
Use the inset map to practise atlas skills. Children look at the copymaster first, then practise finding York on different maps.

Old walls and gateways are a good subject for artwork. Make rubbings of bricks and walls to create a collage (link with art).

Combine with Copymaster 8 to make a picture of old and new places (link with history).

Use the picture to discuss preservation of old buildings (link with environmental education).

Copymaster 10 (Types of homes)
Blank out the words with correction fluid and ask children to label the drawings (assessment).

Cut out the labels and picture boxes, separate them and use as a matching activity.

Use the picture boxes to illustrate the horizontal axis of a bar graph on types of homes your class live in (link with maths).

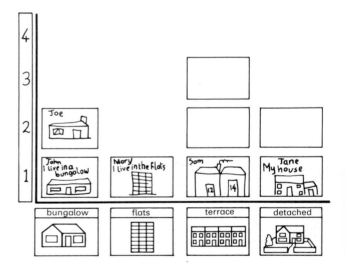

Use the pictures and their labels to start or add to a geography vocabulary/dictionary.

DIFFERENT PLACES

The three places in this section could be used to start a study of a locality in the UK or in another country (in this case France) and compare it with the children's home town.

Wembury
Wembury is a village in South Devon by the sea. It is close to the city of Plymouth and is used by Plymothians for weekend trips. There is a sandy beach with an estate of holiday cabins in a wooded valley 500 metres above it (Churchwood Valley Holiday Cabins). There are rock pools at low tide and miles of cliff walks. In rough weather surf boards can be seen riding the waves. Much of the shoreline is managed by the National Trust, who run the small gift shop and car park. Parts of the cliffs and foreshore have been designated sites of special

scientific interest. Common birds to see include rock pipits, oyster catchers and curlews. Shells found are mainly periwinkles, topshells and cowries. Plants include thrift, pennywort and seaweeds such as channelled wrack, knotted wrack and bladder wrack.

The village is a mixture of old stone cottages and houses and more modern homes, mainly bungalows, some of which are second holiday homes. The school is modern. There is a pub, an hotel, a post office and three or four shops. Wembury is a farming area with cattle, pigs and sheep which graze the headland in summer. Many people who live in Wembury work in Plymouth. Wembury Parish Council produce a useful book called *Wembury Parish – Illustrated Footpath Guide Book*, that contains a footpath map, photos and history of the village and Mewstone Island. Contact the Parish Council (Wembury, Plymouth, Devon) for details.

Copymaster 11 (This is Wembury in Devon)
Use the scene to answer the question 'What is this place like?'

Compare the copymaster with your local area.

Practise atlas skills using the inset and then a larger map to aid children in locating places.

Start a class map of the UK using Wembury as the first marked place.

Colour the scene and make it into a large postcard.

Copymaster 12 (Picture map of Wembury)
Cut out the word boxes and stick them on or around the map to mark the features shown.

The children could follow a footpath route describing the places they pass on the way (link with English).

A class or group guidebook could be made, highlighting the features on the map, with each child making a picture page or written piece to go in the book.

Copymaster 13 (Plan of Wembury)
Use the plan here and the picture map on Copymaster 12 together to identify places.

Blank out the word boxes and use the symbols to make a key for the map, with children writing their own labels.

Make a large map of a small area, e.g. the beach, and devise new symbols for it.

Look at a local map and find some of the same or different symbols.

Colour the copymaster in sections – the village, the beach and coast, the chalets, farmland and sea. Make a colour key.

Copymaster 14 (Holidays at Wembury)
Cut out the picture boxes and use them to head pages in a holiday brochure.

Ask children to choose a picture box and make a poster or postcard about that activity.

Use a selection of the picture boxes to write a story about a holiday.

Use some of the picture boxes to start an investigation using library reference books, e.g. rock pools – 'What is found in them?' (link with English and environmental education).

Cut out the picture boxes and stick them next to your own pictures of items from your local area – decide whether the activity is similar or different (assessment). For example, make a page labelled 'Here' on one side and 'There' on the other. Under 'Here' put pictures of your local birds; under 'There' put seabirds from Wembury.

Copymaster 15 (People at work in Wembury)
Cut out the job names and stick them on to the picture boxes.

Cut out all the boxes and use them as an activity to match people with their places of work and the labels that describe their jobs.

Cut out all the boxes and mount them on card to make a game of Pelmanism, matching places to jobs. The rules are as follows: Put all the cards face down on the table. The first player turns over two cards. If they match, the player keeps that pair and has another turn. If the cards do not match then the player turns them back over and the next person has a turn. The winner is the player who collects the most pairs of cards

Consider jobs in your local area. Are these jobs similar or different to those shown on the copymaster? (Assessment.)

Cut out the picture boxes and use them for data handling. For example, put the jobs into two sets or make a Venn diagram that shows that some jobs can be done indoors and/or outdoors – teacher, waiter, farmer (link with maths).

Stevenage
Stevenage was built in 1946 as one of a number of post-war new towns. It was planned around an existing settlement to relieve overcrowding in London, 50 kilometres away. Stevenage, like many other new towns, has a pedestrianised shopping precinct. As well as shops it contains a cinema, sports centre, library, church and hotel. In the housing estates, walkways and cycle paths are totally separate from vehicular roads. Underpasses allow pedestrian access all around the town. A well-developed road system links all the housing areas with the town centre. Each neighbourhood has its own schools, and there is a large open park and an area of lakes for recreation. Stevenage is close to the A1(M) and has good rail links with London and north to Edinburgh. Luton airport is 13 kilometres away. Local industries include British Aerospace and computer and electronic systems manufacturers; there are also food and wine warehouses.

Copymaster 16 (This is a town called Stevenage)
Use the set of copymasters on Stevenage to study a locality in the UK and compare it with your home town. (This set can be used in a topic on your local area if you live in Stevenage.)

Colour each building differently and then colour the word boxes to match.

Collect postcards or photos of your home town and create a similar composite picture.

Cut out the labels and stick them on the picture as a matching activity.

Copymaster 17 (Picture map of Stevenage)
Use for a geography skills exercise – trace a route describing the places you pass in order.

Draw one simple route and put in your own pictures of people at work, at school or enjoying leisure time.

Use with Copymaster 16 to match places in the picture to places on the map. Use the cut-out word boxes from Copymaster 16 to label this map.

Colour code the different areas of the town. Use different colours for the centre, roads, housing estates and industrial areas.

Copymaster 18 (Plan of Stevenage)
Use with Copymaster 17 to match the places on the picture map with those on the plan drawing.

Make an acetate copy of this copymaster and place it over Copymaster 17 to match places. This acetate can be used separately or in conjunction with the above activity.

Use the picture boxes to make a key. Cut off the words and let the children identify the symbols (assessment).

Copymaster 19 (Things to do in Stevenage)
Cut out the picture boxes and stick them around one of the Stevenage sheets (Copymasters 16–18), joining the activity in the box to the place where it can be done.

Use the cut-out picture boxes to make a sequenced story of a child's weekend in Stevenage (link with English).

Compare the amenities in Stevenage with those in your local town.

Use the pictures as a basis for a large group collage to show 'Things to do in Stevenage' (link with art).

Copymaster 20 (Buildings in Stevenage)
Cut out the picture boxes (with or without labels) and stick them around one of the Stevenage sheets (Copymasters 16–18).

Use the pictures to start a book with the title 'Buildings Have Different Uses', asking the questions 'Who uses this building?' and 'For what purpose?'

Compare these buildings with those in your local area and perhaps make pages titled 'Here and There' for classroom display or children's folders, showing the similarities and differences.

Cut off the labels or blank them out so the children can write their own, researching them from the map on Copymaster 17.

Chinon
Chinon is on the River Vienne, a tributary of the Loire, and is a town steeped in medieval history, with an old town that has fifteenth-century buildings and cobbled streets. In 1429 Joan of Arc came to Chinon to tell the Dauphin about her mission to save the kingdom (see below). There is a statue of her on a horse in one of the squares. A château is visible high above the town. Windy streets and a series of steps lead to the gates of this partially ruined castle that contains a museum about Joan of Arc. Around the town are vineyards in this important wine region of France, the Loire valley. North of the château is the forest of Chinon, the setting for the story of Sleeping Beauty which is dealt with on Copymaster 36. The French Tourist Office (178 Piccadilly, London, W1V 0AL) could provide further information, such as pictures and maps.

Joan of Arc
Joan was a French farmer's daughter, born in a small village in 1412 during a time of war against England.

While Joan was growing up a young man called Charles was the Dauphin (heir to the French throne), but another man, the Duke of Burgundy, wanted to rule France. The people of France were split and civil war broke out. During this war the English became involved, hoping to rule France themselves.

By this time Joan was 13 years old. She saw a vision of three saints, who told her she must leave home and go to help the King of France. She heard their voices many times.

In 1428 the Dauphin had fled to a château in the Loire valley at Chinon. Joan travelled from her village to see him – 11 days' ride on horseback – disguised as a man.

At Chinon, although the Dauphin had disguised himself as a courtier, Joan picked him out easily and knelt before him saying 'Gentle Dauphin, I am Joan the Maid; through me you will be crowned King at Reims'. Moved by the young woman's loyalty, Charles agreed to let her ride out from Chinon for battle fully equipped with an army. At Orléans Joan won the fight against the English and the Dauphin was crowned at Reims Cathedral in 1429. But the fighting went on – Joan was captured by people who were afraid of her. They said she was a witch and an enemy of the Church. At her trial she would not deny that the voices she heard came from God and so she was burnt at the stake.

In 1920 she was canonised and became St Joan. On 24 June the people of France have a national holiday in her honour. (For further reference, see *Joan of Arc* by Brian Williams, Cherrytree Books, 1989.)

Copymaster 21 (This is Chinon in France)
Use Copymasters 21–5 as the basis for the study of a locality outside the UK.

Use the inset map to find France and Chinon in an atlas or on a wall-map of Europe.

Colour the picture very simply using blue for water, brown for buildings, green for trees and vines, and appropriate colours for bridges and statues. Make a colour key.

Cut out the word boxes and use them to label the picture.

Use the word boxes for children to label their own drawings of these features (assessment).

Use the coloured-in landscape for the cover of a relevant topic book.

Copymaster 22 (Picture map of Chinon)
Use the map to talk about what this town is like. Ask children if it is similar or different to the place where they live.

Use the French/English words to label the map.

Use the French/English words to start a short dictionary of French words with pictures to illustrate it.

Use the picture boxes at the foot of the copymaster either for your dictionary or to stick on to the map.

Copymaster 23 (Plan of Chinon)
Use this plan with the map on Copymaster 22 to practise map-reading skills, by matching the pictures on the one to the symbols on the other.

Make an acetate copy of this copymaster to put over the map on Copymaster 22 and match up the features. This can be a separate activity or used in conjunction with the above.

Trace a route with your finger (e.g. from the campsite to the château) and make your own simple map with pictures or symbols.

Blank out the numbers before photocopying the copymaster and ask children to label the plan, using the picture map on Copymaster 22 for reference (assessment).

Copymaster 24 (Places to see in Chinon)
Use the large picture to explain how castles are built in defensive positions (link with history).

Tell the story of Joan of Arc (see page 4). She came to Chinon to tell the Dauphin about her mission to save the kingdom.

Compare this château with a castle near you or with a famous castle anywhere in the United Kingdom.

Use the historical aspects of the small pictures in conjunction with work on how life used to be in the fifteenth century – a project on clothes could link in here.

One of the small pictures could start a postcard design and encourage the writing of the child's impression of this place.

Most towns have statues – the picture on the copymaster could start a statue trail in your home town, visiting a series of statues to find out some local history.

Copymaster 25 (At work in Chinon)
Non-fiction about France is becoming easier to find for young children – the pictures on this copymaster together with some relevant books could be used to start a research corner.

Children could write their own small book about life in this part of France using cut-outs from the copymaster to start some of their pages.

The vineyard worker could be compared with a farm worker in your local area. Consider the things grown, tools used, weather worked in, tasks done and the end products.

Try making or just tasting French bread, croissants and pastries. Graphs or Venn diagrams could be made to show the children's preferences (link with data handling/IT).

Cut out the pictures and labels, separate them and use them for a matching activity.

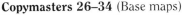

MAPS

Copymasters 26–34 (Base maps)
Use whichever map is most suitable to mark the place you are studying.

These maps could be used by the children to match and mark places they have seen on other pages or on small inset maps in this book.

Use the maps with atlases to find and record the location of places of your choice.

Use the maps to practise marking National Curriculum requirements. One way for children to learn places on maps is for them to *look* at the place on a map, *cover* it up and then *copy* the place on their own map (assessment).

Enlarge the maps for classroom displays.

Make acetates on a photocopier machine so that children can mark the maps (with OHP water-soluble pens or chinagraph pencils) and then rub their work off afterwards to save using paper. You can still photocopy the acetate if you want to keep a record of the work done.

Make worksheets by overlaying the names of places you want the children to mark on the copymaster before you photocopy.

Copymaster 35 (Direction)
Use the word boxes to label the four points of the compass (work with a programmable toy, such as BigTrak, Pip, Roamer or Turtle; link with IT).

Use the copymaster to talk about wind direction and to start a collection of pictures of different types of wind vanes.

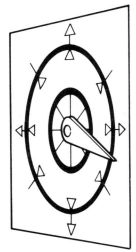

Make a small pointer out of a piece of card and join to the compass with a split pin to make a moving model.

Having shown the children the picture of the weather cock, make wind vanes with different animals and test them out to see which designs work best (link with science and technology).

Copymasters 36–40 (Story and rhyme maps)
The next five copymasters provide picture maps to go with well-known stories and rhymes. The castle in the Sleeping Beauty copymaster is based on the Château d'Ussé, near Chinon in France. You may want to use it in connection with 'Different places', Copymasters 21–5.

Use the copymasters as follow-up activities after telling the story to remind the children of some of the events.

Use the copymasters as picture maps, letting the children mark with arrows or dots the route taken in the story.

Cut out the word boxes and use them to label the pictures.

Let the children tell or write their own version of the story mentioning the features shown on the map (assessment).

Make plan maps of the same routes as those on the copymasters, using symbols instead of pictures and the word boxes as labels for a key.

Use a programmable toy (e.g. Pip or Roamer) to give directions to match the route on the map (link with IT).

After using some of these story maps the children could make similar maps for other stories, such as *Rosie's Walk* by Pat Hutchins or *Mr Gumpy's Outing* by John Burningham.

Use the word boxes to start or add to a dictionary of geographical words, adding the children's pictures to illustrate the pages.

Use the story and a session of colouring in the map as the introduction to a topic. For example:

● the study of a French location or castles (Sleeping Beauty)
● shopping i.e. 'What's in the basket?' (Red Riding Hood)
● farming (Little Boy Blue)
● animals or sport (The Hare and the Tortoise)
● giants or magic (Jack and the Beanstalk).

MAKING THINGS

Copymaster 41 (A bottle of milk)
Use the copymaster to trace the milk's journey from the cow to the supermarket, making a concertina book by taking a long strip of paper and folding it up like a concertina. Open it out and it can stand on the desk, or

be pinned on the wall or hung like a mobile to make an interesting display. Cut out the picture boxes (with or without labels) and use them to illustrate one or both sides of the concertina book, which can have as many or as few pages as you wish.

Cut off the labels and ask children to match them with the appropriate picture or to make up their own (assessment).

Use the labels to stick on to Copymasters 42–4 in this section.

Use the pictures to write a sequenced account as a group or individually (link with English).

Copymaster 42 (At the farm 1)
Colour the different fields according to their use and make a key.

Make separate pictures of all the farm buildings and label them.

Decide which field the cows graze in and trace their route to the milking shed.

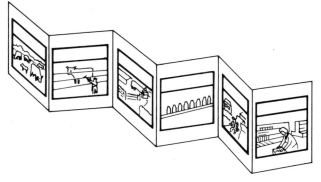
A concertina book

Make a larger map similar to this and use with plastic farm animals to play games, adding routes for the workers on the farm.

Copymasters 43 (The milking shed)
The large picture could be the focus for a discussion on how cows are milked and form the centre of a display of the children's own paintings.

Mark with blue circles the places where water is used (link with health and safety).

Use the labels to stick on to the picture of the milking shed.

Use the small picture boxes for children to illustrate sentences about the milking shed in their own books.

Copymaster 44 (People who provide milk)
Use these pictures with Copymaster 41 for children to make their own topic book on a relevant subject.

Cut out the picture boxes and labels and use them as a matching exercise.

Use the labels to stick on to children's own pictures of the jobs described.

Use with other copymasters in the 'Making things' section (see topic index) to produce a picture bank of people's jobs.

Link with the other farm occupations mentioned in this section to create a fuller picture of work on a farm.

Copymaster 45 (A woollen jumper)
Make a concertina book (see page 6) to show the sequence of events involved in making a woollen jumper.

Cut off or blank out the labels and let children add their own (assessment).

Use picture 4 to start a collection of items or pictures of items made from wool.

Collect wool from fences in a sheep-farming area and compare this raw wool with processed wool (link with science).

Copymaster 46 (At the farm 2)
Talk about the picture with the children. Discuss how sheep have warm woollen coats that allow them to live in cold places and how their sure-footedness allows them to graze on steep hillsides.

Mark the route the shepherd and dog take to the hilltop and the way they bring the sheep into the pen.

Other people use hills for walking. Here is an opportunity to talk about the Country Code (link with environmental education).

Make a map from the picture, using colours or symbols for fields, pasture and hills. Cover with a grid to use for grid reference practice.

Label the picture or the children's own maps with the word boxes.

Copymaster 47 (The wool mill)
The pictures here can illustrate how one sort of building is used and can be compared with a building in your area.

Make a display of the various processes using the pictures. Add pieces of different textures and coloured woollen cloths to the display.

Try weaving or spinning (link with art).

Tell the class about the mills and cottage industries of the past and how technology has changed things (link with history).

Copymaster 48 (Who helps to provide our woollen clothes?)
Stick the word boxes on to the pictures to label the jobs.

Children can choose one picture and use it to illustrate their description of that job.

Cut out the pictures. Hand one unseen to a child and ask them to act out or describe their day at work. The others must guess the job.

Use with copymasters from other pages in 'Making things' to create a reference book on people's jobs.

Copymaster 49 (Strawberries)
Cut out the word boxes and label the plant (link with science).

Colour the plant appropriately, using a reference book or colour-by-numbers key added before photocopying.

Use the copymaster with a minibeast topic showing the importance of pollination (link with environmental education). The bee symbols can be used to decorate children's own pictures and writing.

Use the plant picture as a model for a material or paper collage (link with art).

Copymaster 50 (The strawberry story)
Cut out the picture boxes and make a sequence line showing the strawberry-farming process.

Cut out all the boxes and ask the children to put them in sequence and label them (assessment).

Instigate an activity with one large group or several smaller ones, where each child describes one part of the process in words and pictures.

Grow a strawberry plant in a pot or in the school garden as a class project and monitor its progress (link with science).

Copymaster 51 (The strawberries leave the farm)
Use the picture to talk about a fruit farm and the different fruit grown in this country.

Look at the picture to work out the three places to sell fruit, i.e. the local town, a larger city where it has to be sent, and at the farm shop.

Children can use the fruit symbols to decorate their own pictures, work, maps and workcards.

Write stories about the day a family went to a 'Pick your own' strawberry farm (link with English).

Use the word and picture boxes to label the fields and to make a notice for the farm shop to be displayed in the classroom.

Copymaster 52 (The fruit and vegetable shop)
Colour the fruit and vegetables on the stall, either following a colour-by-numbers key put on the copymaster before photocopying or with children using their own knowledge after a class discussion.

Collect labels from jars and cans to illustrate ways in which fruit is processed.

Visit a local shop and collect current prices to relabel the picture. Ask the question 'Why do prices change at different times of the year?'

Let children make plasticine or clay fruit and display them on a 'stall' in your classroom (a table will do), using some of the pictures in this section to decorate it.

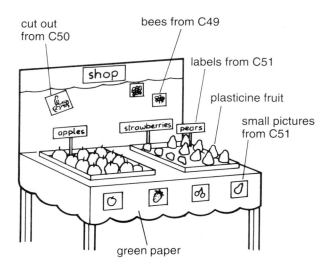

cut out from C50

bees from C49

labels from C51

shop

plasticine fruit

small pictures from C51

apples   strawberries   pears

green paper

Copymaster 53 (Fishfingers)
Cut up the picture boxes and use them (with or without labels) to make a sequenced storyboard showing the journey of the fish from the sea to the supermarket.

Use library books to research different types of fishing boats.

Collect empty fishfinger packets to compare weights when full, size of packet, numbers of fishfingers in each packet, prices and possibly type of fish used (link with maths).

Write a sentence to go with each picture, using the relevant label in the sentence (link with English).

Copymaster 54 (On the fishing boat)
Talk about how it would feel to work on a boat and which jobs the children would like or dislike. Let children paint pictures to go with their answers.

Use the picture boxes around a large outline of a trawler (drawn by the teacher) to mark the different parts of the ship.

Use the pictures to stimulate creative writing about the sounds and smells on board a fishing boat (link with English).

Copymaster 55 (The harbour)
Colour the picture using blue for the sea, another colour for the fishing industry buildings, and another colour again for other buildings.

Talk about the need for a safe harbour. Find other references in this book ('Homes and settlements') on a similar theme.

Take an imaginary walk around the harbour describing what you would see. Ask the children to describe a fishing boat. Move on and ask them to think about the cafe. You could ask the children to tell you who would be having breakfast and why. You could then progress to things the children would hear and smell. Let children transfer their thoughts into written accounts or paintings.

Use an atlas to find some of the harbours around the coast of the UK. You could start with the ones nearest your local area.

Copymaster 56 (Making fishfingers)
Cut out the pictures with their labels to make a concertina book (see page 6) of the fishfinger manufacturing process.

Cut the labels off or blank them out with correction fluid before photocopying, and ask the children to label the pictures (assessment).

Muddle the pictures up and make a sorting activity.

Cook and taste different brands of fishfingers.

Copymaster 57 (A wooden chair)
Use the copymaster as a sequencing activity, by cutting out the pictures (with or without labels) and asking the children to make a story line.

Blank out the labels with correction fluid and ask children to write captions for each box.

Use this copymaster with Copymasters 58 and 59 as role-play stimulus, by asking small groups of children to act out the job in the picture you give them.

Look at the different designs of chairs in your school and continue the sequence on the copymaster with pictures of school chairs drawn by children (link with technology).

Copymaster 58 (In the forest)
After discussion with the class make large pictures of all the fire hazards in a forest.

Add pictures of forest birds and animals to the picture.

Use the picture to find out all the other types of job that are carried out in a forest as well as felling trees.

Use the word boxes to label the picture.

Use the word boxes to start or add to a geography dictionary that includes words and pictures and can be used as a class reference book.

Copymaster 59 (In the sawmill)
Go outside to look at how big trees actually are, then discuss the size of a sawmill and the reasons for using conveyer belts.

Talk about the dangers of working with heavy items, sharp machines and loud noises. Identify the safety precautions taken in the sawmill.

Cut out and stick the safety symbols on the picture where children think they are appropriate (link with health and safety).

Cut out the symbols and stick them on another sheet – write down other places they may be used, or just what they stand for.

Copymaster 60 (Different timber)
Take one box and use it as the label for a display of items made from the timber of that particular tree and specimens of leaves, fruit and twigs.

Choose a tree and go and study a specimen, taking bark rubbings and making leaf prints (link with art/ environmental education).

Use the four boxes to start a tree book. Add other boxes for trees that the children have researched themselves. Easy subjects for study include willow, used for baskets, and balsa, used for models.

Copymaster 61 (Coal)
Use the copymaster as an information sheet and discuss the coal-making process with the children.

Use an old fish tank to make a real model of coal formation. Layer twigs, sand and water in the fish tank, and arrange them as in the lower left illustration on the copymaster. Complete the display by using the pictures and/or captions to label the tank.

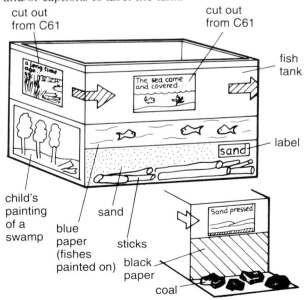

Blank out the words with correction fluid and let the children write their own captions.

Use the copymaster as an introduction to a topic on rocks or energy (link with science).

Copymaster 62 (Under the ground)
Use the copymaster as an information sheet and discuss what it would be like to work in a mine.

Write about a day in a miner's working life, using the pictures for illustration and ideas.

Use history reference books to compare mining methods in early times with today (link with history).

Copymaster 63 (Safety in a mine)
As a technology activity, let children design their own models of the helmet and Davey lamp and use them with overalls to add a new costume to the class dressing-up box.

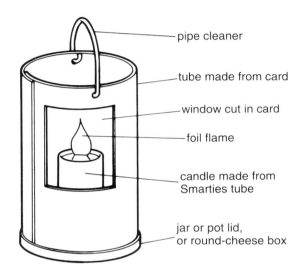

Make a life-size picture of a miner, using the copymaster to help with the design.

Compare the old Davey lamp with the new battery lamps. (A museum will often loan one.)

If your school has science equipment for making electric circuits, use it to show how a miner's head-lamp is lit (link with science).

Copymaster 64 (How coal is used)
Let the children use the copymaster to find out what coal is used for.

Blank out the labels with correction fluid and ask children to write the captions.

Use the pictures to make simple workcards that ask the children to find out something from a book you have in the library.

Discuss the problem of pollution from coal smoke (link with environmental education).

Copymaster 65 (Bricks start here)
Identify the large earth-moving machines and link them up with toys the children may be able to bring in.

Stick the safety symbols from Copymaster 59 (In the sawmill) on this page to show the dangers of quarries (link with health and safety).

9

Use the copymaster as a book cover to start a project on soils, homes, buildings or machines.

Use the word boxes to label the machines.

Copymaster 66 (The brickworks)
Cut out the pictures (with or without labels) and let the children put them in sequence.

Blank out the labels with correction fluid or cut them off and ask children to describe the brick-making process.

Cut out the three pictures of bricks being made and baked. Glue them inside a large outline picture of a brickworks factory (drawn by the teacher) to make a class display.

Mount each picture (with or without label) on card with a relevant question for the children to research or answer. For example, 'What is this building used for?' or 'What is a kiln?' (Assessment.)

Copymaster 67 (A building site)
Cut out the word boxes and use them to label the picture.

Colour the different materials being used on the site and make a colour key.

Use this copymaster to discuss buildings and all the jobs related to building. Children could add drawings of any jobs not shown.

Use the copymaster as an observation sheet on a walk that passes a building site, with children ticking or colouring the jobs they notice that are also on the sheet.

Copymaster 68 (A new house)
Join the material labels with a line to the relevant features of the house which are made from them (link with science).

Cut out the picture boxes and stick them around the house next to matching items.

Use the picture boxes for data handling. Venn diagrams could show which materials are used for these objects (link with maths).

Colour the house using a different colour for each material.

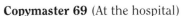

PEOPLE WHO HELP US

Copymaster 69 (At the hospital)
Use the pictures (with or without labels) with other relevant copymasters (see topic index) to make a topic book about jobs.

Blank out the job titles with correction fluid or cut them off so children can write their own (assessment).

Use the copymaster as an information resource for children to find out about a hospital.

Cut up the copymaster and divide the pictures between a group of children, letting each child write about the job they have been given, to compile a group book.

Copymaster 70 (Hospital buildings)
Use the picture as a reference to make 3-D model buildings and a signpost which the children can play with, and lead on to a talk about hospitals.

Mark routes on the map for people visiting different parts of the hospital.

Talk about the different buildings and the things that go on in them.

Stick the pictures from Copymaster 69 (with or without labels) around this picture, joining each job to the place you would find it with a line. Add others the children know or can find out about.

Copymaster 71 (At the fire station)
Use the picture to talk about the fire service with the children.

Let children make a list of all the things needed at a fire station.

Use the picture of the fireman as a model for a life-size collage.

Cut out the picture boxes and stick them on a separate sheet for the children to label or write sentences about.

Copymaster 72 (Getting to the fire)
Cut out the arrows and stick them on the map, showing the fire engine's route.

Make a plan map of the route using symbols for the buildings and make a key.

Write an account of the fire engine's route, putting the things it passes in the correct order (assessment).

Add the fire and 999 labels to the map and use the copymaster as an introduction to a discussion on making emergency telephone calls.

Copymaster 73 (The police)
Use the pictures as a resource for the children to find out about the jobs police officers do.

Ask the children to suggest what may be happening in each picture (link with English).

Ask different groups to take one scene and develop a short role play about what is happening.

Link the topic with a visit from your local constabulary, who will tell the children about other jobs – the children can then extend the copymaster in their own way.

Copymaster 74 (Police transport)
Use the pictures one at a time to write short stories about a police officer's job.

Use the copymaster with a project on transport to illustrate children's work.

Cut out the pictures and make a concertina book (see page 6) with children's writing added.

Make about 12 copies of the copymaster, cut out the pictures and make a game of snap.

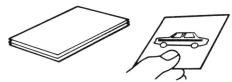

Snap!

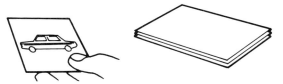

MOVING AROUND

Copymaster 75 (Road signs)
Discuss road safety with the children, using this copymaster.

Use the copymaster to motivate the children to make a road safety poster, concentrating on one aspect of the picture (link with art).

Use the picture boxes to start a sheet of road symbols. The children can add ones they spot in the neighbourhood.

Mark the picture with red sticky spots in all the danger areas (link with health and safety).

Copymaster 76 (The bus station)
Let children make a list of all the people you can see in the picture and record what they are doing.

Colour all the passengers one colour and the people working another colour.

The children could use the picture to write a sequence of instructions for using a bus station.

Use the picture to set up an imaginary bus station in the classroom or playground. Use the area for role play.

Copymaster 77 (On the motorway)
Use the picture to talk about motorways and to compare them with local roads. Discuss why we need motorways.

Colour the various types of vehicles on the motorway in different colours and make a key.

Use the first row of picture boxes with Copymaster 75 to make a collection of road signs.

Use all the picture boxes to make your own motorway view.

Copymaster 78 (On the Underground)
Colour all the items above the ground one colour and the items below the ground another.

Cut off the street scene from the copymaster and let the children create another picture of life above ground.

Use the copymaster with the sheet on London ('Homes and settlements' Copymaster 7) to make a 'Travel around London by Underground' picture.

Use the copymaster to talk about what it is like underground and as a stimulus for creative writing (link with English).

Copymaster 79 (At the airport)
Use the copymaster as a reference to make a larger floor plan of an airport, using this with toy trucks and planes in play sessions.

Cut out the labels (with or without pictures) and stick them on to the picture.

Cut out the picture boxes and stick them on a separate sheet for children to write their own labels.

Use the picture boxes in a project book on people's jobs, together with pictures from copymasters in other sections of this book (see topic index).

Copymaster 80 (At the railway station)
Let children list all the jobs done at a railway station.

Use the Royal Mail picture box as part of a project on the postal service.

Use the copymaster on a visit to a station as an observation sheet, letting children mark the things noticed. Find out which towns you can go to directly from your nearest station. Put these towns on a map.

Use the picture boxes to illustrate work on the things that happen on trains.

Copymaster 81 (Transport)
Make a count of traffic in your local area. Children can stand in a safe, supervised place and count the number of cars, lorries, vans, bikes etc. that pass over a short period of time. Use the picture boxes on the copymaster to illustrate a bar graph of the data collected (link with maths).

Sort the picture boxes into types of transport that take place on roads, rail and in the air.

Sort the picture boxes according to the different types of power used – electricity, petrol (and diesel if you choose) and muscle (link with science) (assessment).

Use the picture boxes for children to trace and make their own transport scenes.

WATER IN THE ENVIRONMENT

Copymaster 82 (Where we find water)
Get the children to colour all the water blue and the other features appropriately as a skills exercise in colour-coding and map-making techniques.

Cut out each picture box (with or without label), use it as a title to a page and stick similar pictures cut out from travel brochures underneath.

Use each picture to write a sentence that describes the scene. This could be an activity using a dictionary, with children looking up the definition of each water word and writing it down by their picture.

Make several photocopies of the copymaster, cut out the picture boxes, mount them on card and use them to play snap.

Copymaster 83 (Journey to the sea)
Use the copymaster as a discussion opener to help the children use and understand geographical vocabulary.

Cut out the picture boxes (with or without labels) from Copymaster 82 and make a wall display using this page as a reference.

Talk and then write about a journey from source to sea – it could involve a drop of water or a boat.

Blank out the labels with correction fluid, then photocopy the copymaster for the class or group, asking the children to label all the parts of the river (assessment).

Make a plan map from the picture, with children either working as a group making a large floor map or individually. Pictures or symbols could be used to show all the places on the river.

Copymaster 84 (Water comes and goes)
After a discussion about the water cycle add arrows to show water movement.

This copymaster could be used as the precursor to an evaporation experiment. Leave saucers of water or wet cloths in cool, hot and draughty positions and observe where the most drying takes place (link with science).

Mark or colour the places where water is found on the copymaster.

Finish the account of what happens in the water cycle. Discuss the questions 'What happens to the snow?' and 'Where does rain go when it reaches the ground?'

Copymaster 85 (Pond creatures)
Use the copymaster as an identification sheet when visiting a pond (link with environmental education).

Let children trace or copy the creatures on the sheet for their own work.

Use the small boxes as a tick list during a pond visit, or for illustrating a graph of the numbers of creatures seen (link with maths/IT).

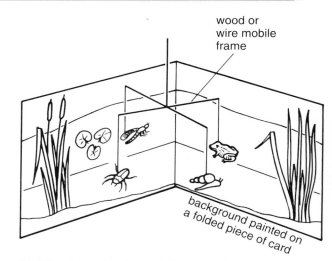

wood or wire mobile frame

background painted on a folded piece of card

Mobile with animals made from card or C85

Use the copymaster as a stimulus for artwork. Enlarge the pictures to make pond mobiles or use the design as a reference to make a 3-D pond model.

Use the boxes to sort out which part of the pond the various creatures live in. Put them into the following sets: On the 'surface', 'In the pond', 'On plants' and 'On stones'. Venn diagrams could be used here (assessment).

Copymaster 86 (Water plants)
Colour the copymaster following numbers you have added to the plants before photocopying. Use pink for thrift and water lily; yellow for iris; purple for sea holly; brown for bulrush and seaweed; white for frogbit; and green for pondweed and duckweed.

Use the copymaster as an identification sheet out of doors or for specimens brought into the school.

Add small boxes to the copymaster for the children to tick when they see the plants on a visit (link with environmental education).

Use the copymaster as a basic reference for a large-scale piece of collage art.

Copymaster 87 (Water birds)
Cut out the birds from the copymaster and give them to the children to make an individual or group collage of a lake.

Colour the copymaster using library reference books to find the correct colours (link with English).

Add tick boxes for the children to use during an appropriate visit.

The outlines of the birds can be used for tracing to add illustrations to the children's own work.

Discuss the sort of habitat these birds need. Think about their need for food and shelter (link with environmental education).

Copymaster 88 (Water transport)
Cut out the large pictures from several copies of the copymaster and mount them on card to make a game of snap.

Discuss what the boats are used for. Use the small picture boxes as a sorting activity, letting children group them into pleasure and working boats (assessment).

Cut out the large pictures and use them to illustrate a frieze about water transport.

Use the small picture boxes to illustrate a graph showing the answers to the question 'Who's been on a … ?'

Copymaster 89 (Fun on the water)
Use the copymaster as a reference for artwork. It could be the basis for painting, model making or a group collage.

Use the copymaster as a tracing sheet to help the children with their drawing.

Use the small picture boxes for science work on wind, human and motor energy. Cut out the boxes and sort them according to which sort of power is used (link with science) (assessment).

Use the picture boxes for illustrating a graph on the types of energy needed to propel boats (link with maths).

Copymaster 90 (Using water)
Use the copymaster as a vocabulary-learning exercise, letting children label their own pictures with the small picture boxes (the blank box is for the children's own ideas).

Use the picture boxes to start a data-collection exercise – make a survey sheet to record how many times and for what purpose the family uses water in a day.

Use the main picture to introduce a discussion in health and safety on 'When should we wash our hands?' The children could make a poster on this theme, using the parts of the copymaster that they want.

Let children stick the picture boxes on drawings of their own houses to show where these activities take place.

WEATHER AND CLIMATE

Copymaster 91 (Make a weather record)
This copymaster contains two types of weather chart: the top chart is the simpler, for use with children aged around five years old; the bottom chart involves more complex skills and is suitable for children aged around six and a half years old. The top chart is also suitable for older children if it is used with the large picture boxes from Copymaster 92. (Link with science.)

Use the chart at the top of the copymaster to record the daily weather, cutting out the picture boxes (with or without labels) or children's own pictures and sticking them on the appropriate day.

The large picture boxes and symbols on Copymaster 92 will also fit the chart at the top of the page.

In the blank spaces at the bottom of each column in the top chart stick the labels 'sun', 'rain', etc. or let the children copy down the day of the week.

Monday	Tuesday	Wed	Thursday	Friday
Sun	rain	rain	cloud	cloud

Day	Weather	Temp °C	Rain
Monday		11°	—
Tuesday		10°	✓
Wednesday		9°	✓

The small picture boxes showing symbols on Copymaster 92 will fit the bottom chart on this page, which can be used to record temperature as well as the weather.

If the temperature is not being recorded, the title of the second column in the bottom chart can be blanked out with correction fluid. This and the third column can then be used to record rainfall (amount or just 'yes/no'), wind direction or a change in the weather.

Photocopy more copymasters for a longer period of record-keeping.

Copymaster 92 (The weather chart)

All the large picture boxes fit the simple chart on the top of Copymaster 91, so the two copymasters can be used together. (Note that large symbols with labels are not intended for use with the chart on Copymaster 91, but can be used for general information.) The small symbols can be used with the lower chart on Copymaster 91. (Link with science.)

The large picture boxes and symbols can be cut out and mounted on card to make matching games like snap and Pelmanism (for the rules see page 3).

The pictures or symbols (small and/or large) could be used in a child's own design of a weather chart (assessment).

Copymasters 93–6 (Spring, Summer, Autumn and Winter)
These four copymasters can all be used in similar ways.

Make a seasons book with all four copymasters, adding children's writing and their own paintings and drawings (link with English).

Make large pie charts (either one large one, or a separate one for each season), sticking the small picture boxes in the correct season (assessment).

Take one feature for study (e.g. trees) and see how it changes throughout the year (link with science/environmental education).

Use the small picture boxes, cut out and mounted on card, to make a game for guessing 'Which season?'

Use the four copymasters when talking about people's jobs, using the farmer as an example of a person whose job changes with the seasons.

Use the pie charts to aid learning of the months of the year.

Match the picture boxes to the main pictures with lines or by cutting and sticking.

Copymasters 97, 99, 101 (Living in the Arctic, Living in a desert, Living in a rainforest)
These three copymasters can be used in similar ways and together.

Colour code the pie charts, choosing 'cold' and 'hot' colours.

Make a pie chart for the UK (link with work on seasons).

Use the pictures to illustrate written accounts of life in other climates.

Design a tourist guide describing visits to these places.

Copymasters 98, 100, 102 (Arctic plants and animals, Desert plants and animals, Rainforest plants and animals)
These three copymasters can be used in similar ways and together.

Use the copymasters with the corresponding ones on 'Living in …' (Copymasters 97, 99, 101) to make topic books or large poster-type pictures.

Use the copymasters to encourage further reference work with school library books (link with English).

Use the copymasters with an atlas to mark on a wall map the places where these climates are found.

Collect as many of the plants shown on the copymasters as possible (several are obtainable here as indoor plants, e.g. Swiss cheese plant) and use the pictures as labels.

LOOKING AT THE LAND

Copymaster 103 (Mountains)
Use the scene in the copymaster to discuss what this place is like, and who lives in and who visits mountain areas.

Compare this scene with a picture of your local area.

Use the copymaster as a stimulus for creative writing about a mountain adventure or in the form of a walker's notes on the things seen (link with English).

Use the picture boxes to make a holiday diary; each one could start a day's record of activities.

Stick the picture boxes around the scene to match them with the leisure activities shown.

Copymaster 104 (Hills)
Compare the copymaster with other scenes in this section. Ask the questions 'How is it the same?' and 'How is it different?'

Cut out the word boxes and let children use them to label the picture on the copymaster or a picture of their own. The blank boxes can be used to make new labels.

Use the copymaster as a design for a wall collage (link with art).

Use the labels to start a picture dictionary of geographical features, with children either working individually, or together to make a class reference book.

Copymaster 105 (The coast)
Colour the sea, the rock pools and the stream blue and the other features appropriately as a skills activity.

Discuss the action of the sea, referring to the arch, the broken cliffs, the high-tide line and the groyne.

Use the rock pool inset together with library reference books to discover more about life in the sea (link with English).

Use the high-tide line inset to talk about pollution and for children to head their own work on litter. The picture could stimulate children to collect items washed up by the sea if they are near or visiting the coast (link with environmental education).

Copymaster 106 (The countryside)
Use the copymaster as a vocabulary-matching exercise, drawing lines from the word boxes to the relevant parts of the picture.

Blank out the word boxes and ask children to label the features (assessment).

Use the copymaster with a group to discuss the Country Code and make it into a poster.

Make a large map of the area shown on the copymaster and add on the footpath route and children's own pictures of the features. The small word boxes could be used to label the map.

Copymaster 107 (Marshes)
Compare the copymaster with other pictures in this section or with your local area. Assess the similarities and differences.

'Who uses the marshes?' Different paintings of these people, animals and birds could circle the copymaster and make a wall display.

The small picture boxes (and/or labels) can be cut out and added to the picture or used as illustrations for the children's own writing.

Wildlife conservation – use the picture to discuss how some habitats are important for birds and animals and may need protecting. The RSPB (The Lodge, Sandy, Beds., SG19 2DL) will send you information on wetlands and birdlife. Compare birds in the school grounds with the birds in marshes, e.g. herons, mallards, reed warblers, marsh harriers and kingfishers (link with environmental education).

A village in the countryside

shop	house	road	church	farm

A village by the sea

| harbour | caravans | cafe | beach | village |

A village in a mining valley

village	pit	hills	church	football ground

A market town

bus	car park	shop	post box
church	cafe	bank	market
pavement	telephone	stall	flats

A town near London

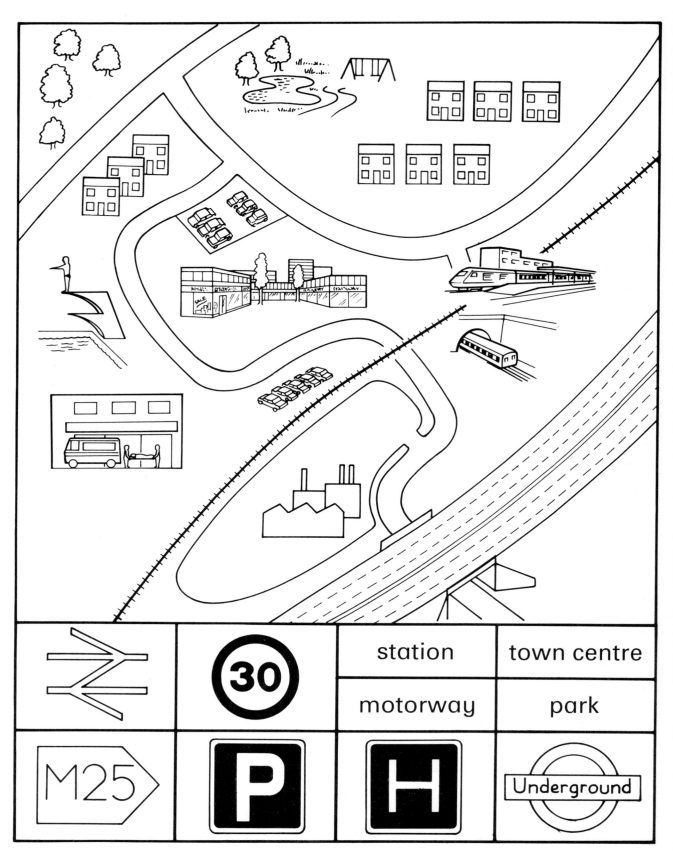

		station	town centre
	30	motorway	park
M25	**P**	**H**	Underground

A new town

A capital city – London

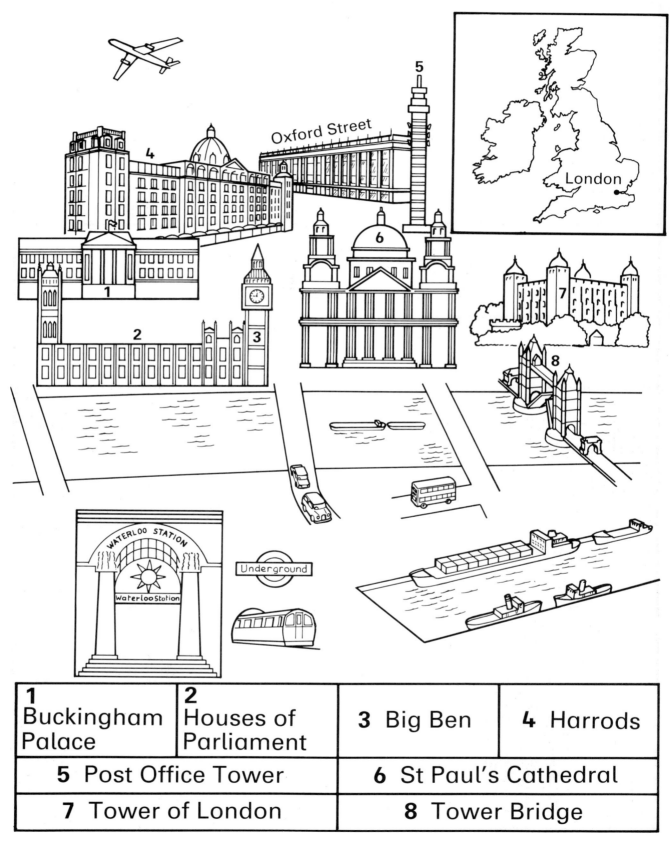

1 Buckingham Palace	2 Houses of Parliament	3 Big Ben	4 Harrods
5 Post Office Tower		6 St Paul's Cathedral	
7 Tower of London		8 Tower Bridge	

A modern city – Plymouth

Plymouth

Plymouth was built again after the war.

Some old buildings are still there.

An old city – York

Old walls circle the city of York.

The cathedral is called York Minster.

Types of homes

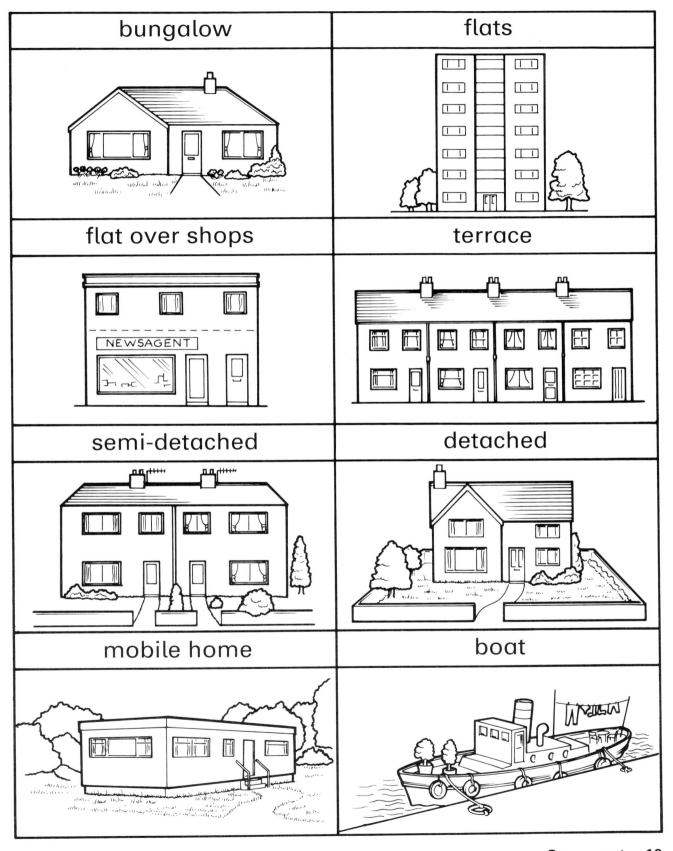

bungalow	flats
flat over shops	terrace
semi-detached	detached
mobile home	boat

This is Wembury in Devon

Wembury

CAFE

Picture map of Wembury

footpath

road

stream

chalets	church	island	cliffs	cafe
stables	toilets	bridge	beach	car park

Plan of Wembury

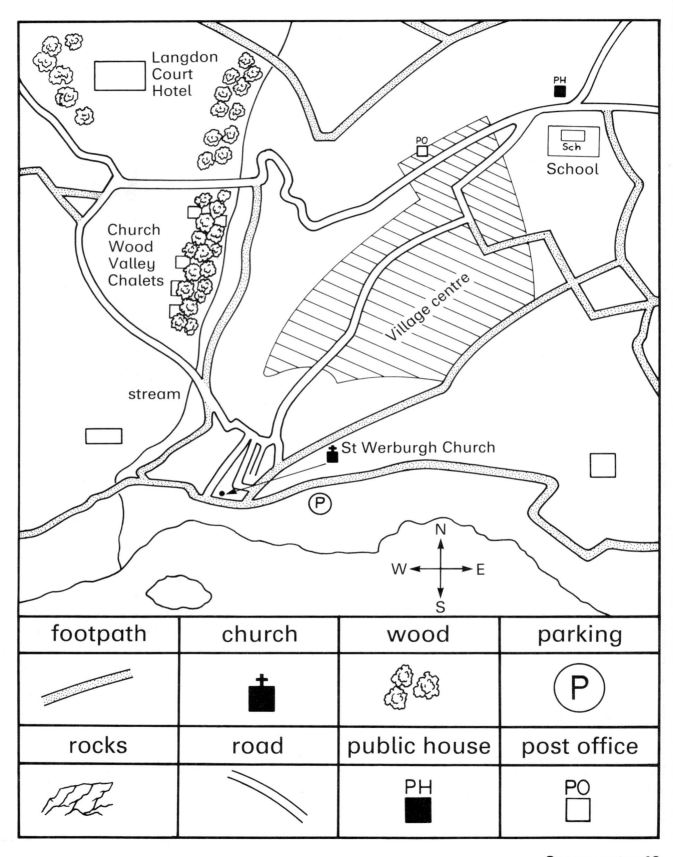

Langdon
Court
Hotel

Church
Wood
Valley
Chalets

stream

Village centre

PO

PH

Sch
School

St Werburgh Church

(P)

N
W   E
S

footpath	church	wood	parking
	†		(P)
rocks	road	public house	post office
		PH	PO

Holidays at Wembury

People at work in Wembury

teacher	car park attendant	vicar	shopkeeper
groom	farmer	waiter	guest-house owner

This is a town called Stevenage

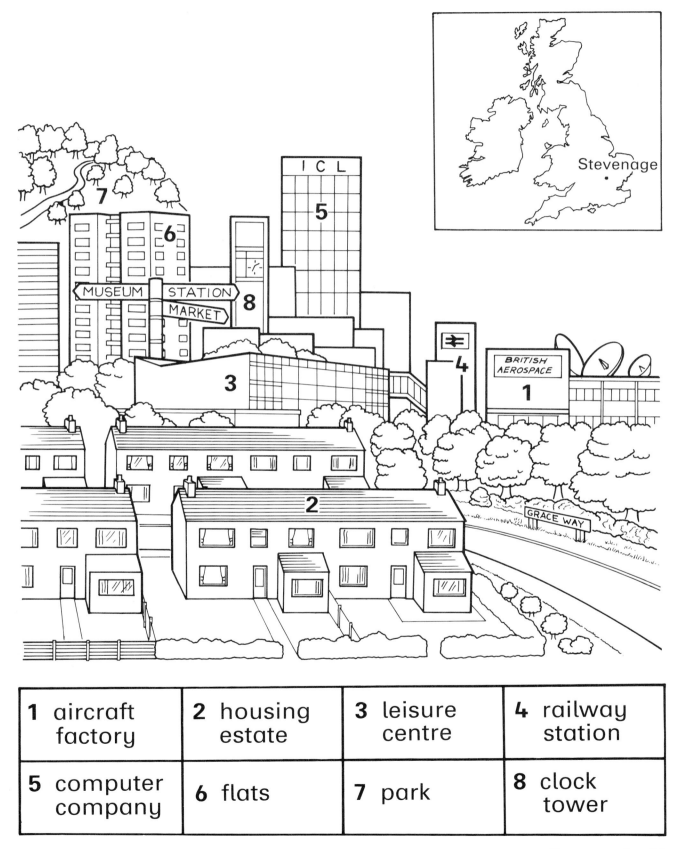

1 aircraft factory	2 housing estate	3 leisure centre	4 railway station
5 computer company	6 flats	7 park	8 clock tower

Picture map of Stevenage

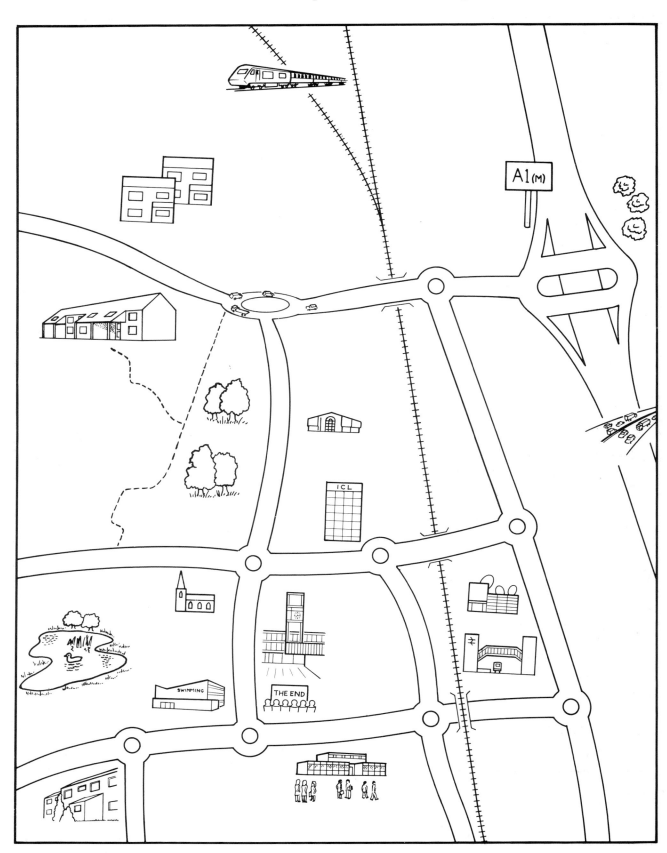

A1(M)

ICL

SWIMMING

THE END

Plan of Stevenage

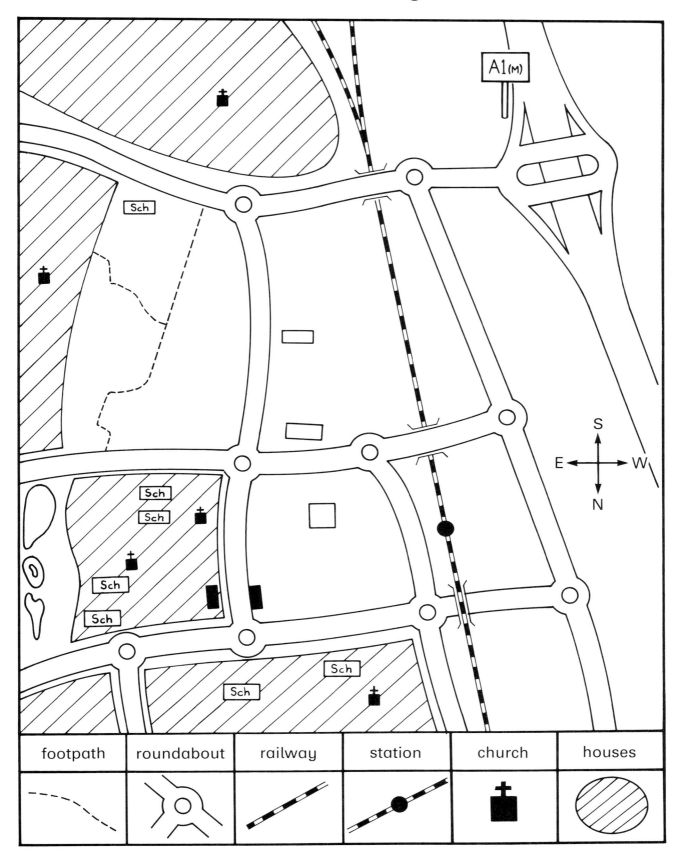

footpath	roundabout	railway	station	church	houses

Copymaster 18

Things to do in Stevenage

Buildings in Stevenage

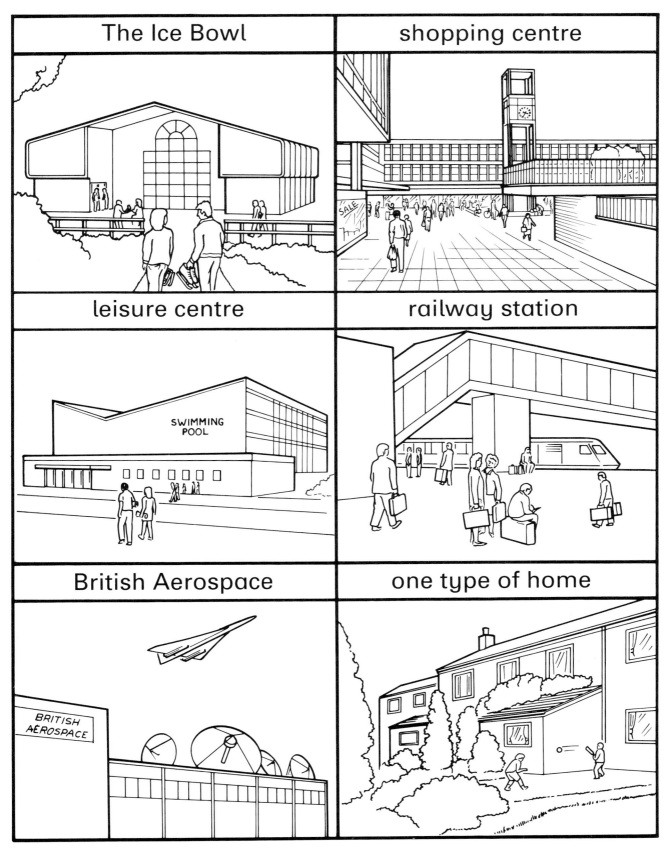

The Ice Bowl

shopping centre

leisure centre

railway station

British Aerospace

one type of home

Copymaster 20

This is Chinon in France

| château | church | vines | bridge | island | town |

Picture map of Chinon

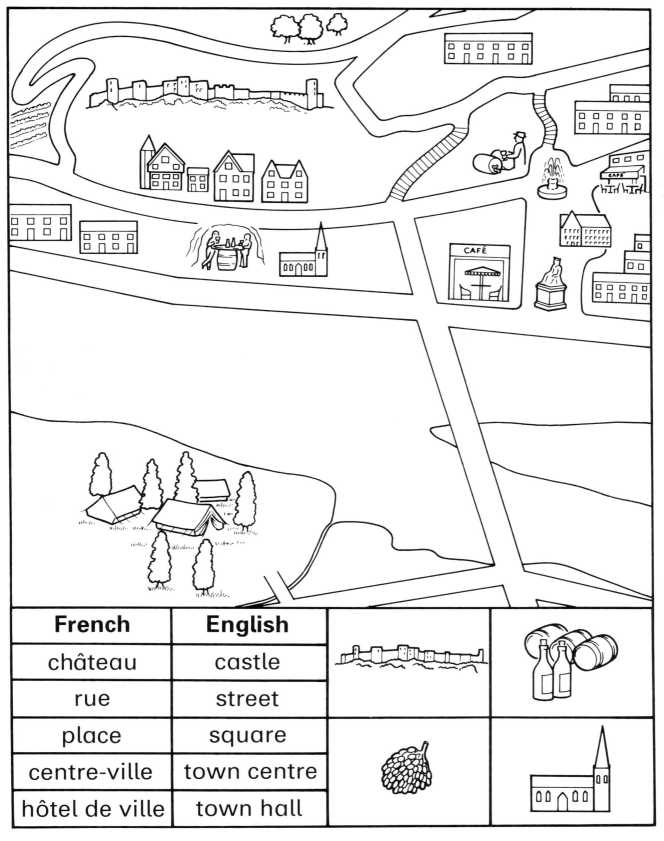

French	English		
château	castle		
rue	street		
place	square		
centre-ville	town centre		
hôtel de ville	town hall		

Plan of Chinon

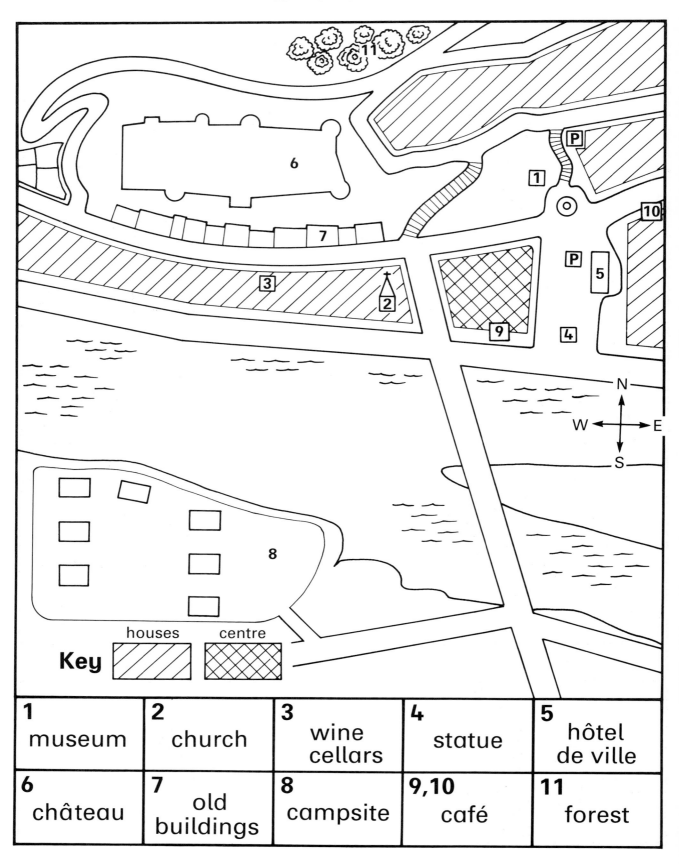

1	2	3	4	5
museum	church	wine cellars	statue	hôtel de ville
6	**7**	**8**	**9,10**	**11**
château	old buildings	campsite	café	forest

Places to see in Chinon

How it was

Nowadays

| château museum | swimming pool |
| tourist train | Joan of Arc |

At work in Chinon

vineyard worker

teacher

shopkeeper

baker

waiter

basket maker

United Kingdom map

N

0   50   100 km

United Kingdom with country boundaries

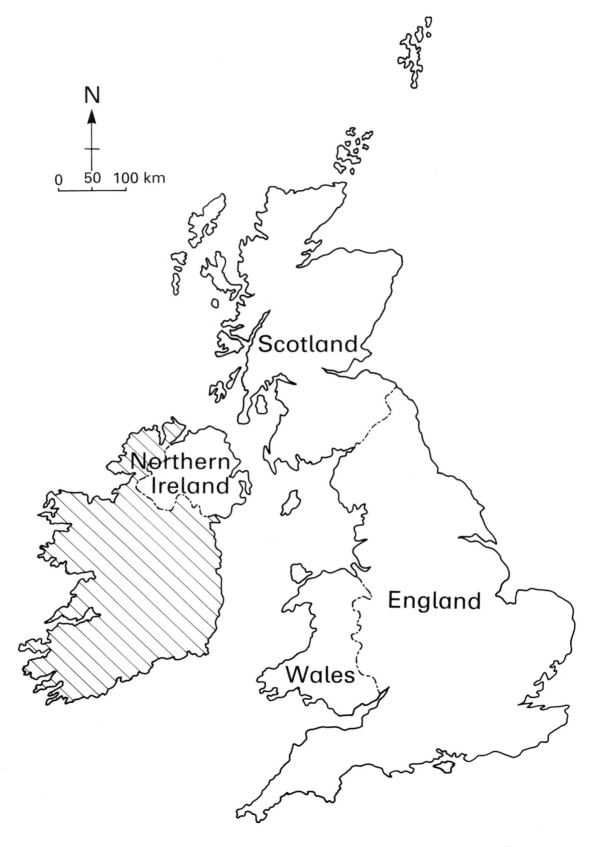

N

0   50   100 km

Scotland

Northern
Ireland

England

Wales

British Isles

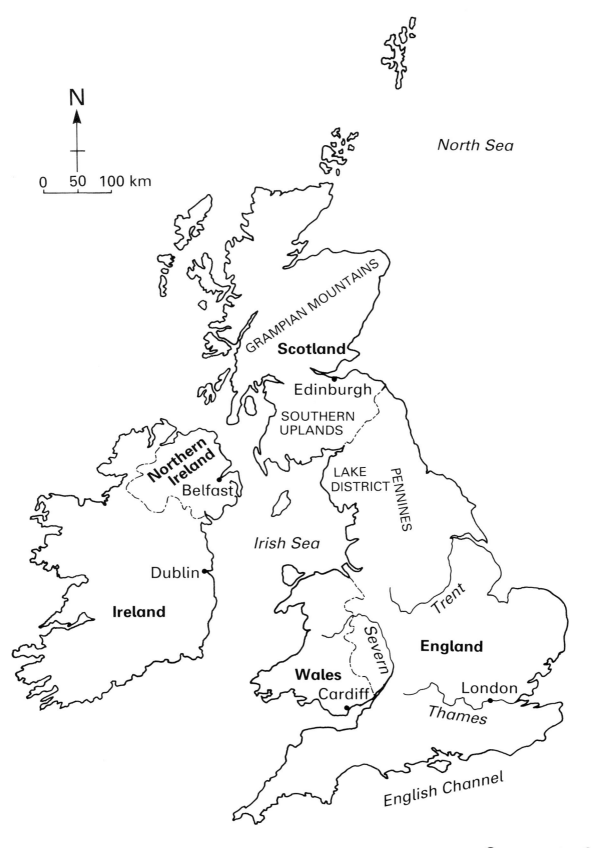

N

0   50   100 km

North Sea

GRAMPIAN MOUNTAINS

Scotland

Edinburgh

SOUTHERN
UPLANDS

LAKE
DISTRICT

PENNINES

**Northern
Ireland**

Belfast

Irish Sea

Dublin

Ireland

Trent

England

Severn

Wales

Cardiff

London

Thames

English Channel

Wales

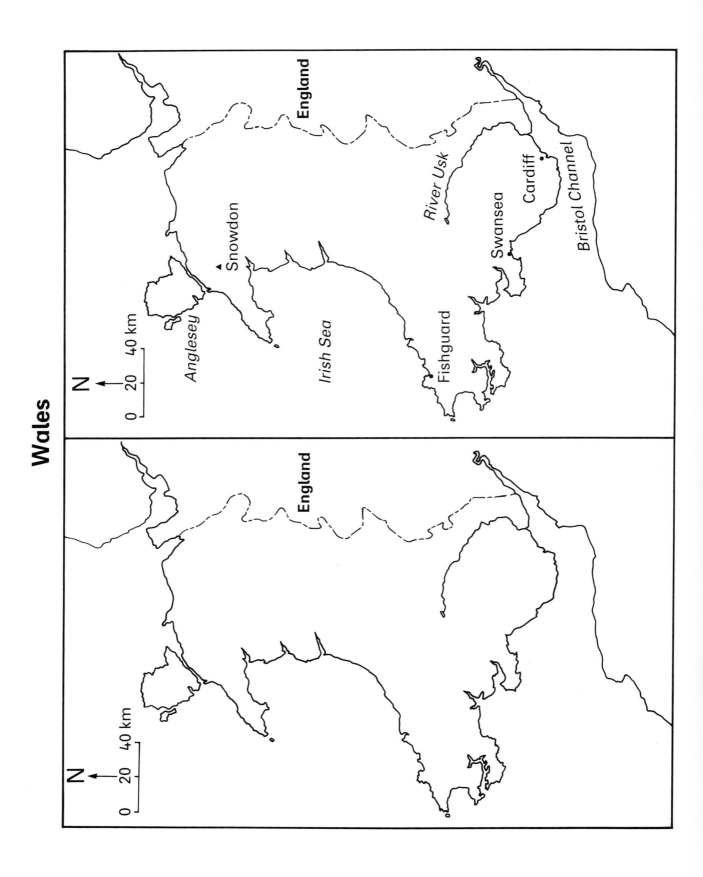

Scotland

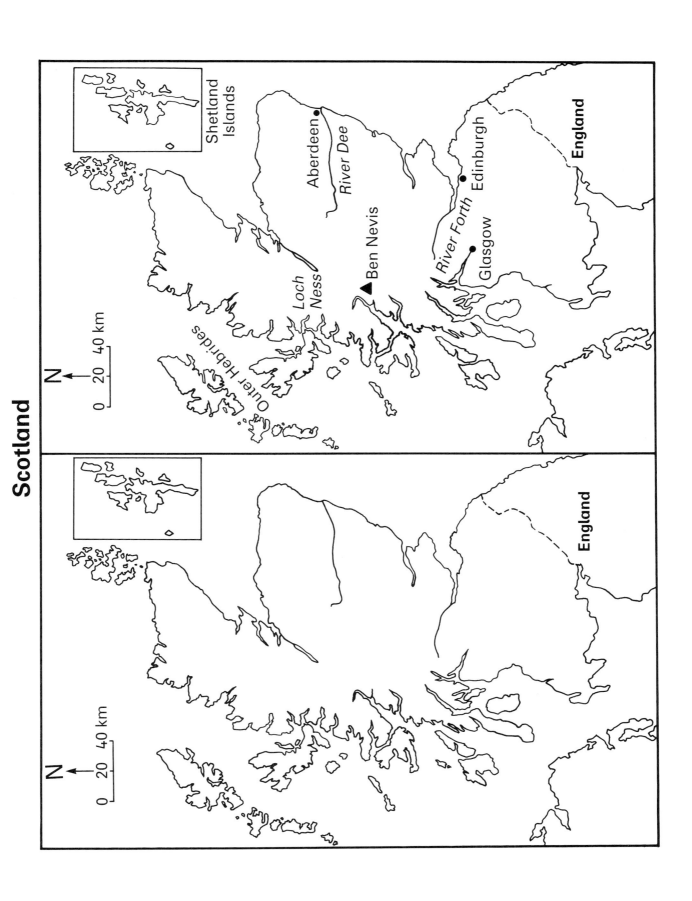

Shetland Islands

Aberdeen

River Dee

Ben Nevis

Loch Ness

Outer Hebrides

River Forth

Edinburgh

Glasgow

England

N

0 20 40 km

England

N

0 20 40 km

Copymaster 30

Great Britain

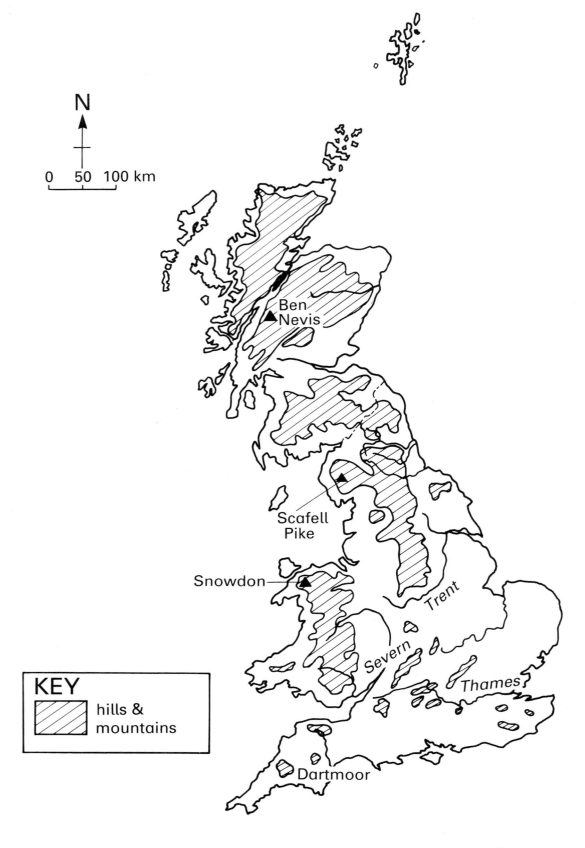

N

0 50 100 km

Ben
Nevis

Scafell
Pike

Snowdon

Trent

Severn

Thames

KEY

hills &
mountains

Dartmoor

Northern Ireland

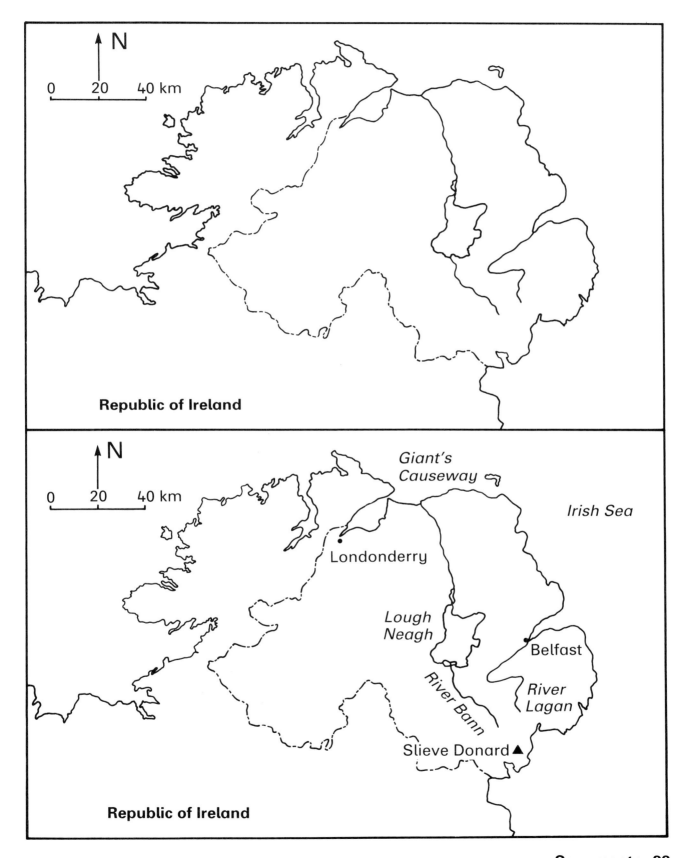

Republic of Ireland

Republic of Ireland

World map

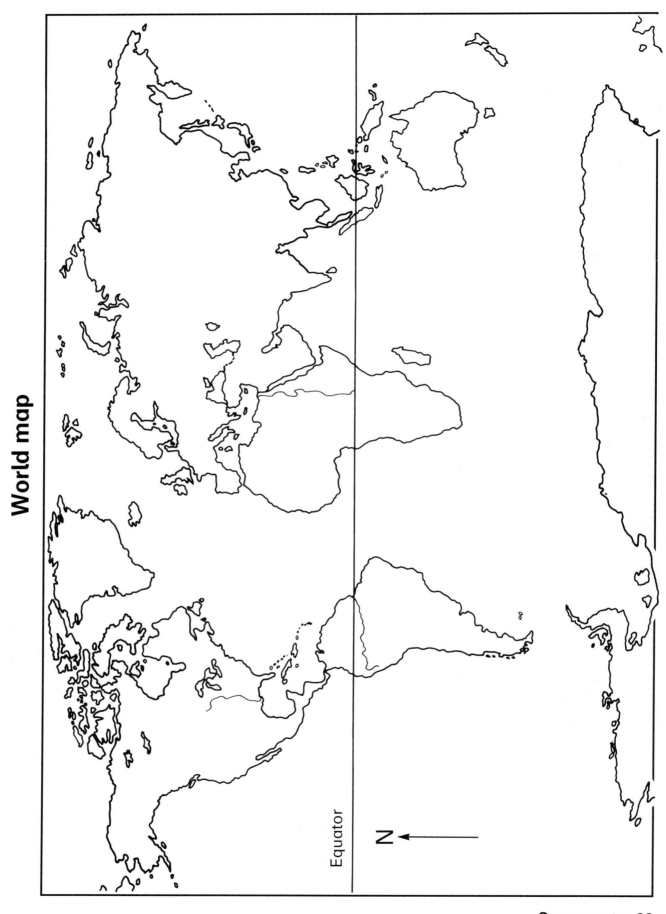

Equator

N ←

World map with names of continents and oceans

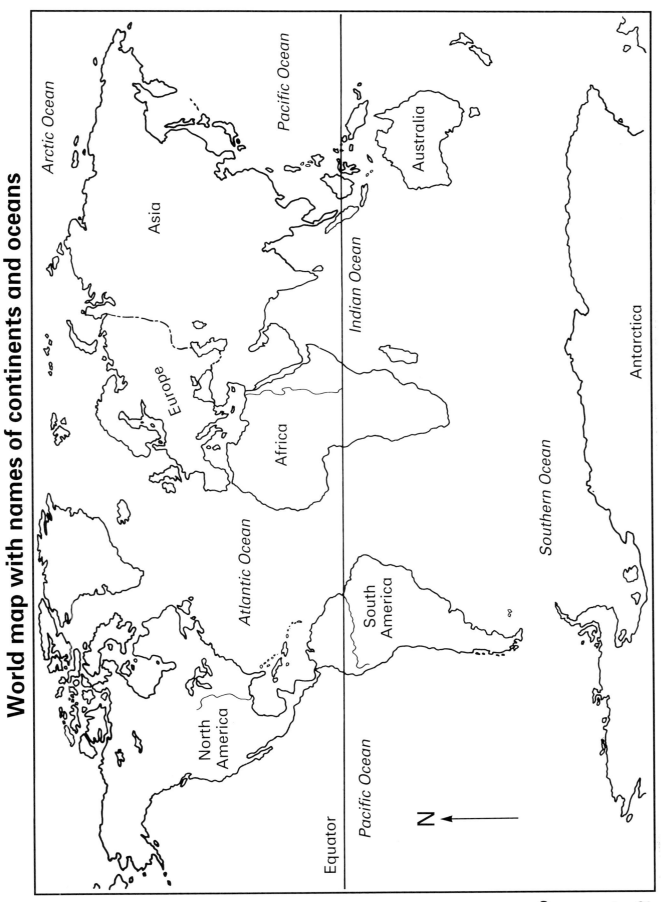

Direction

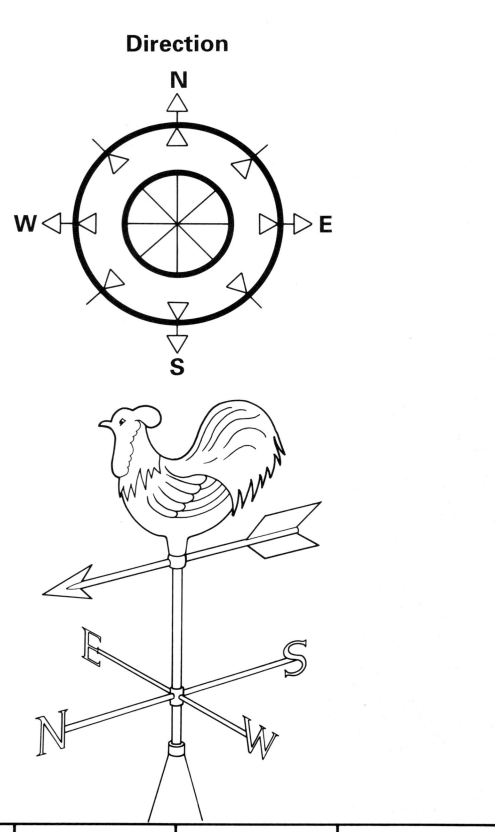

north	south	east	west

Sleeping Beauty

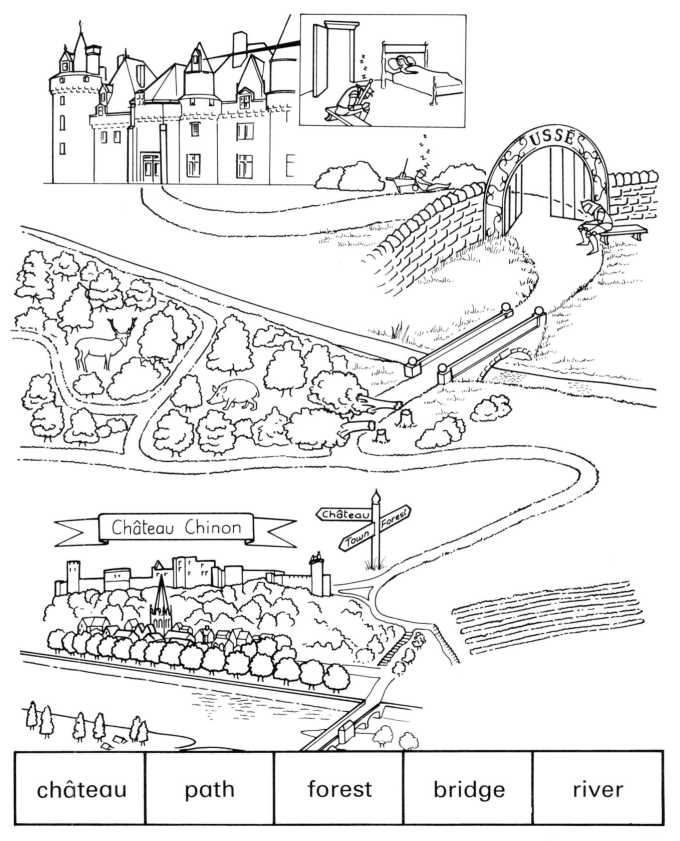

| château | path | forest | bridge | river |

Red Riding Hood

| wood | path | cottage | shop | meadow |

Little Boy Blue

| meadow | cornfield | haystack | gate | stile |

The Hare and the Tortoise

| bridge | river | wood | path | field |

Jack and the Beanstalk

| market | village | shop | road | castle |

A bottle of milk

1 In the field

2 At the farm

3 A milk tanker

4 At the dairy

5 Buying milk

At the doorstep

In a shop

At the farm 1

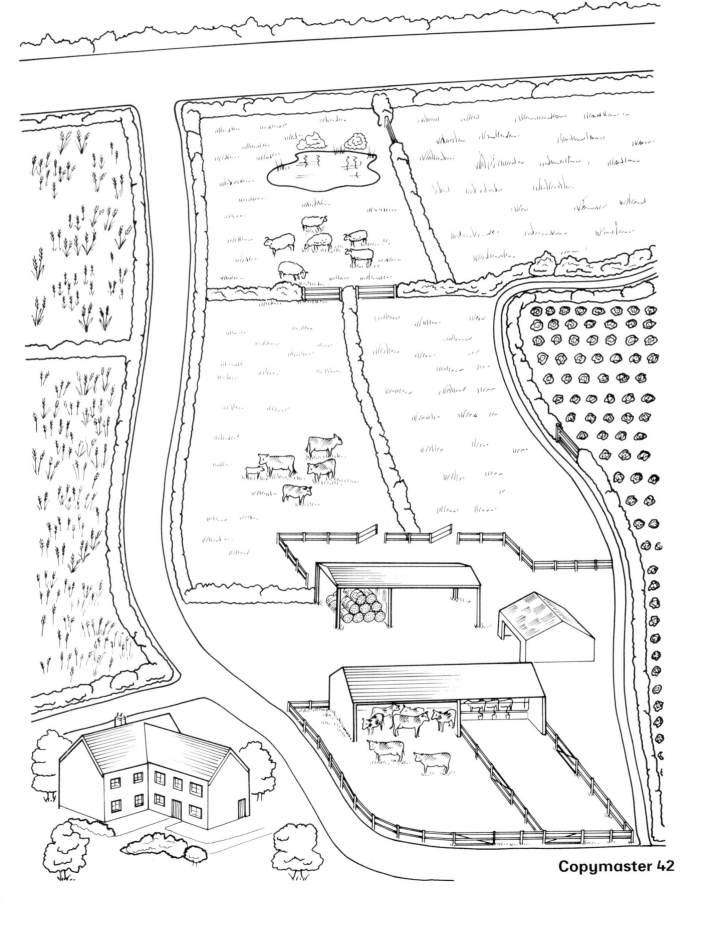

The milking shed

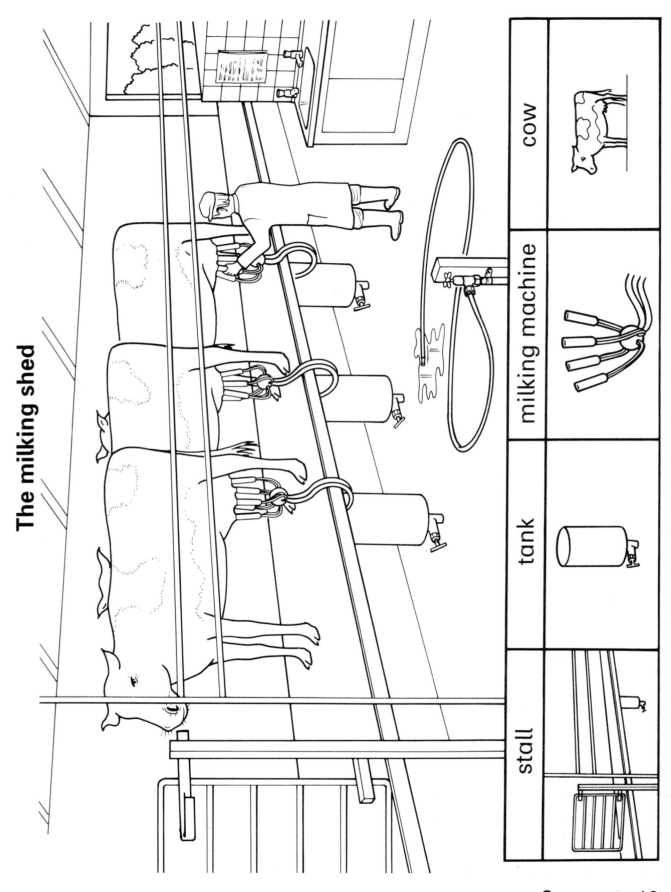

stall	tank	milking machine	cow

People who provide milk

the farmer	the dairyman
the tanker driver	the milkman

A woollen jumper

1 Sheep at the farm	2 Shearing
3 At the wool mill	4 A woollen jumper

At the farm 2

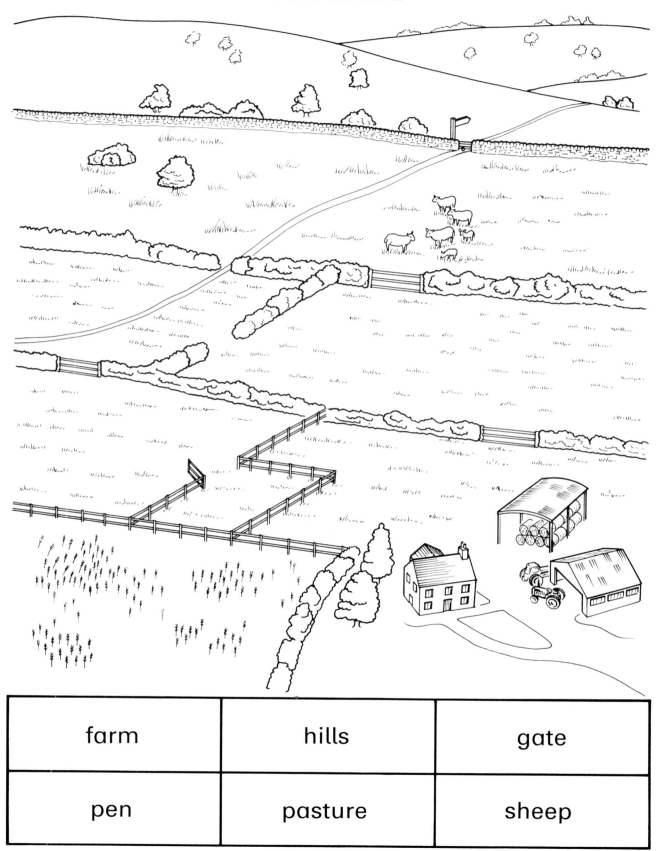

farm	hills	gate
pen	pasture	sheep

The wool mill

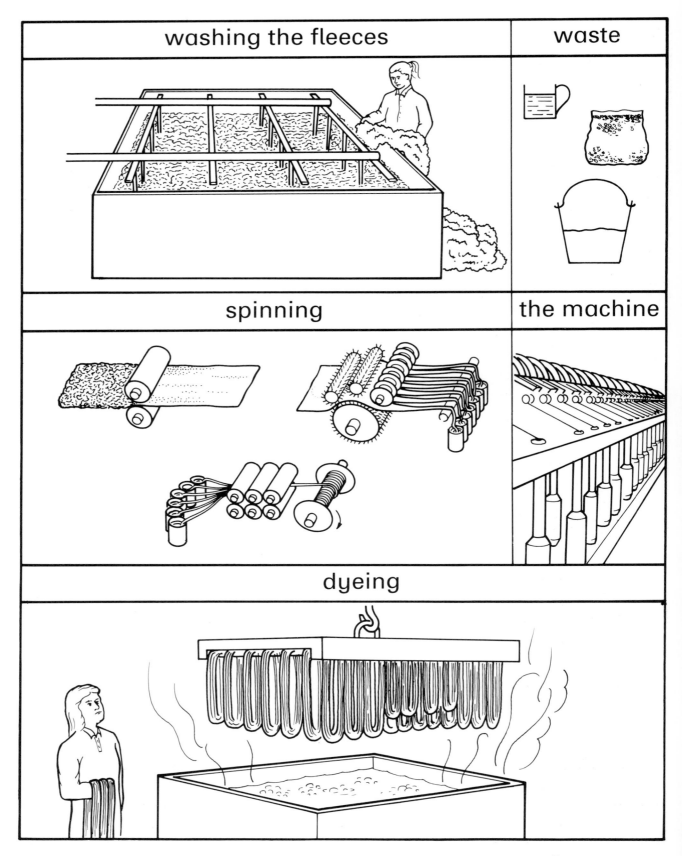

washing the fleeces

waste

spinning

the machine

dyeing

Who helps to provide our woollen clothes?

| shepherd | shearer |
| mill worker | shopkeeper |

Strawberries

flowers	leaves	bees	
fruit	runner		

The strawberry story

1 planting	2 growing
3 picking	4 packing
5 transporting	6 selling

The strawberries leave the farm

strawberries	pears			P.Y.O.
apples	cherries			shop

The fruit and vegetable shop

Fishfingers

1 Catching fish

2 At the fish market

3 In the factory

4 In the supermarket

On the fishing boat

on deck

the bridge

echofinder

radio

the galley

The harbour

Making fishfingers

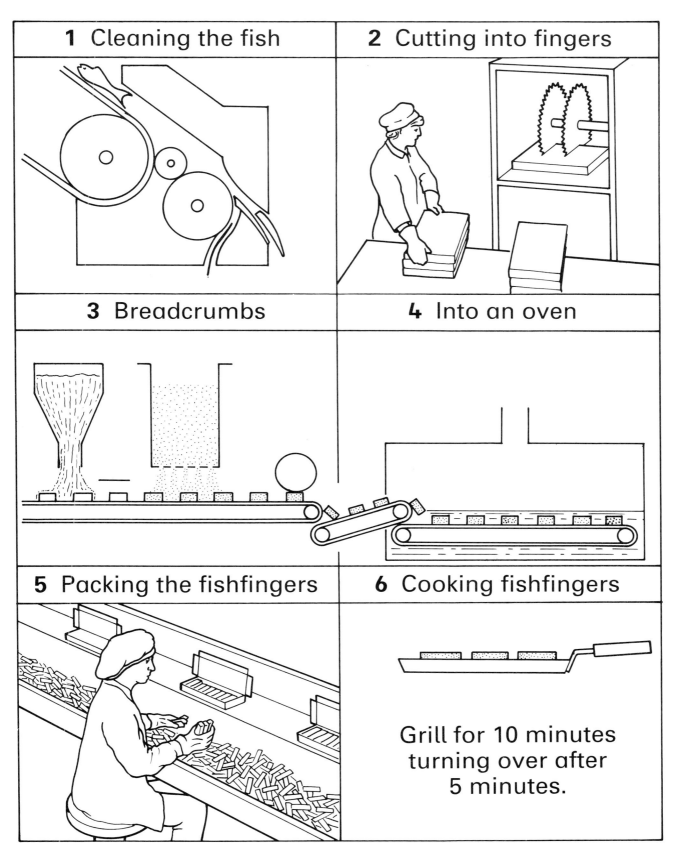

1 Cleaning the fish

2 Cutting into fingers

3 Breadcrumbs

4 Into an oven

5 Packing the fishfingers

6 Cooking fishfingers

Grill for 10 minutes
turning over after
5 minutes.

A wooden chair

1 In the forest

2 Transporting trees

3 The sawmill

4 The carpenter

In the forest

logs	forester	felling	tree guards
forest	fire break	transporter	fire beaters

In the sawmill

Use ear protectors

Different timber

oak

beech

larch

pine

Coal

A long time ago ... (300 million years) there was a swamp.

The sea came and covered the tree trunks.

Sand pressed on the trunks and made them into coal.

sea

sand

←tree trunks

All this took millions of years.

Under the ground

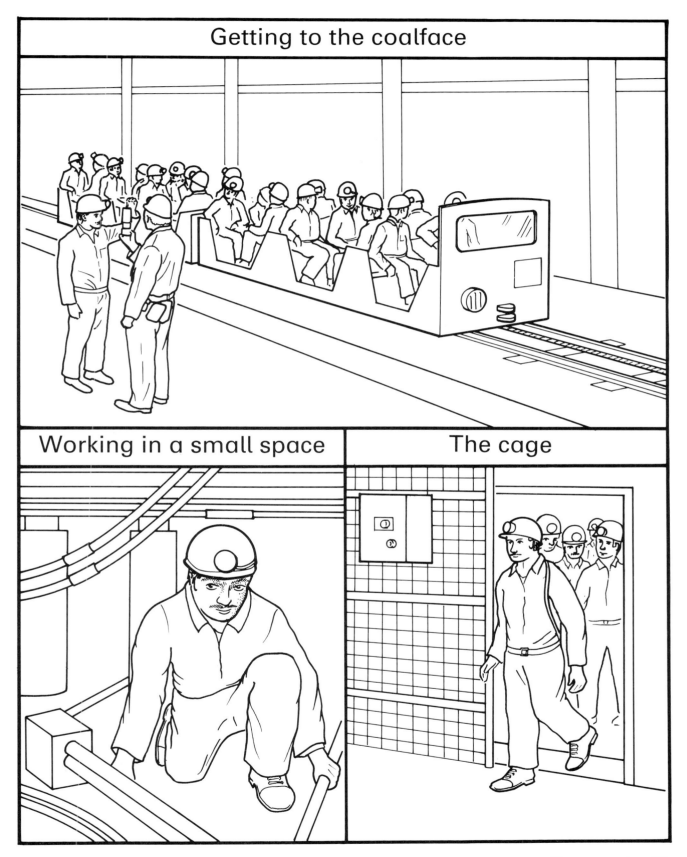

Getting to the coalface

Working in a small space

The cage

Safety in a mine

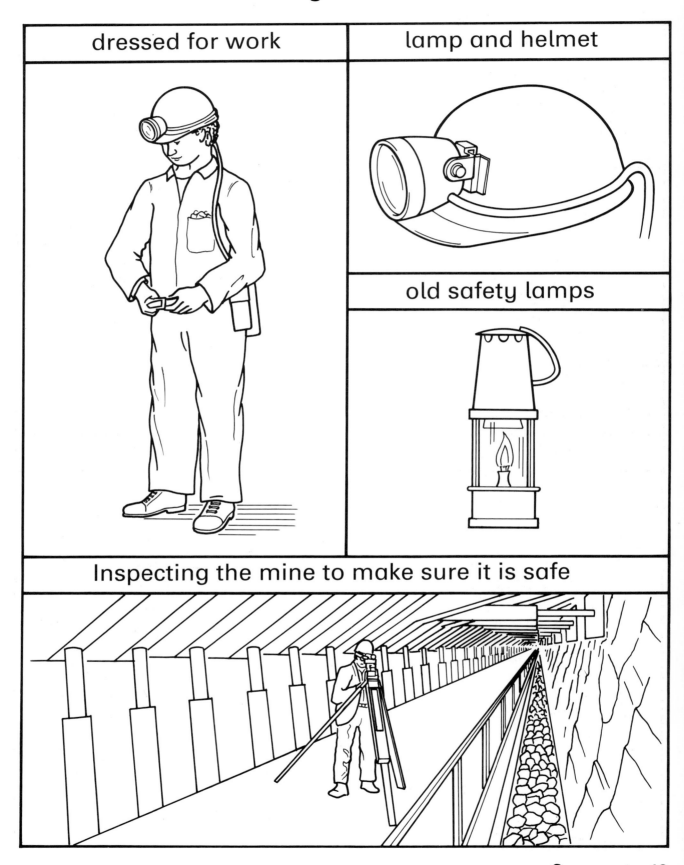

dressed for work

lamp and helmet

old safety lamps

Inspecting the mine to make sure it is safe

How coal is used

to heat homes

to make electricity

to help make steel

in steam trains

Bricks start here

digger	bulldozer	dumper

The brickworks

The clay arrives

Some bricks are made by hand

Most bricks are made by machine

The bricks are baked in the kiln

LONDON BRICK Co.

A building site

bricks	walls	scaffolding	hard hats
tiles	roof	ladder	digger

Copymaster 67

A new house

clay

clay

glass

metal

wood

wood

metal plastic

concrete

clay

At the hospital

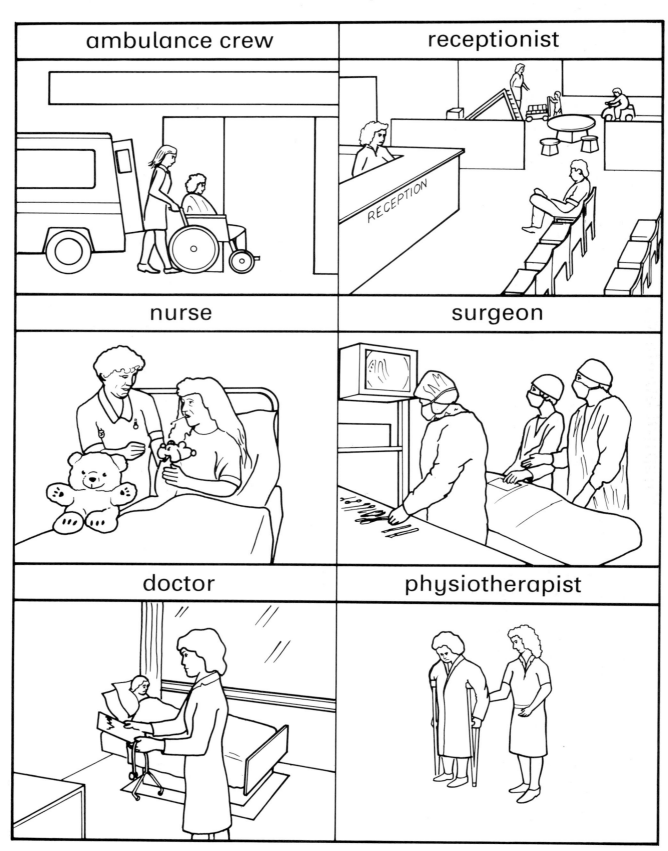

ambulance crew

receptionist

nurse

surgeon

doctor

physiotherapist

Hospital buildings

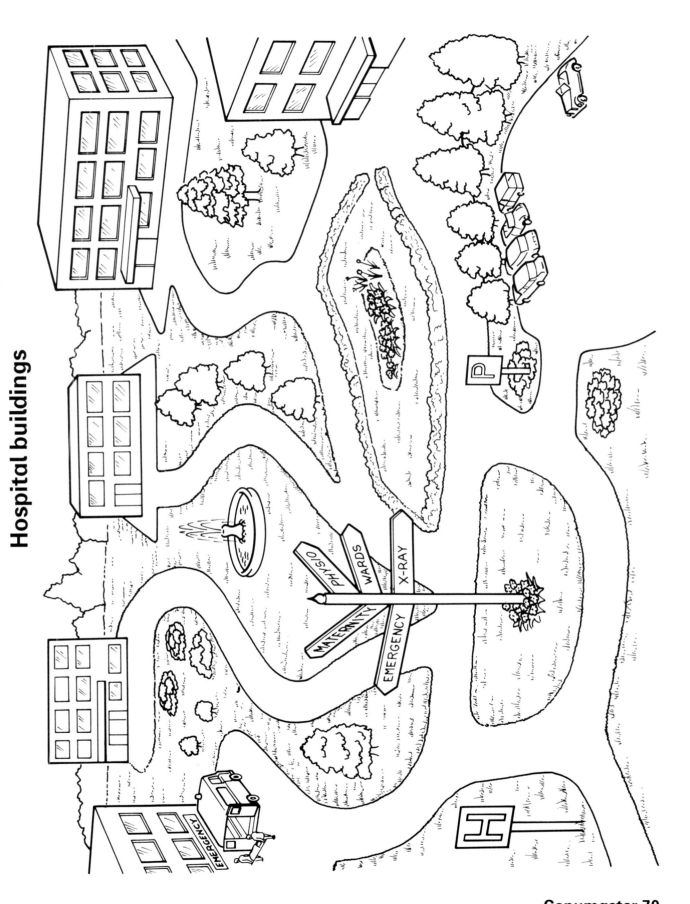

Copymaster 70

At the fire station

Getting to the fire

The police

In the street

On the roads

Solving crime

Police transport

Road signs

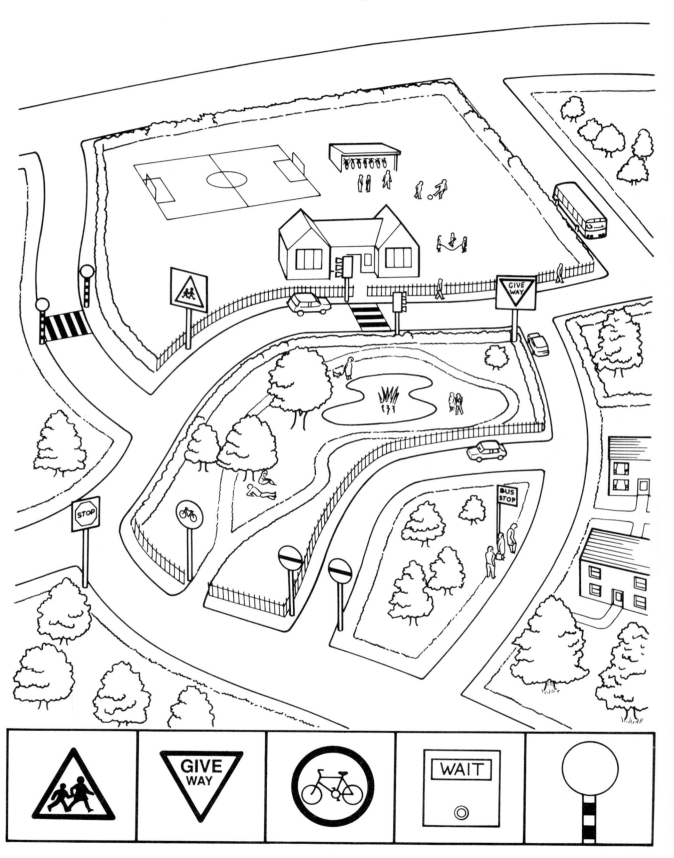

The bus station

On the motorway

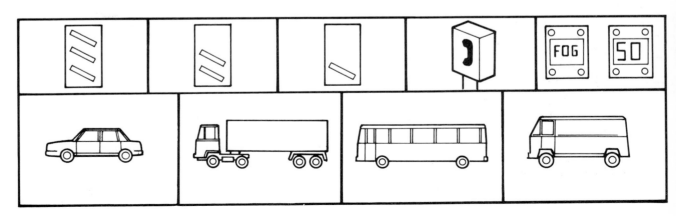

On the Underground

At the airport

| control tower | taxiway | air crew | baggage |

At the railway station

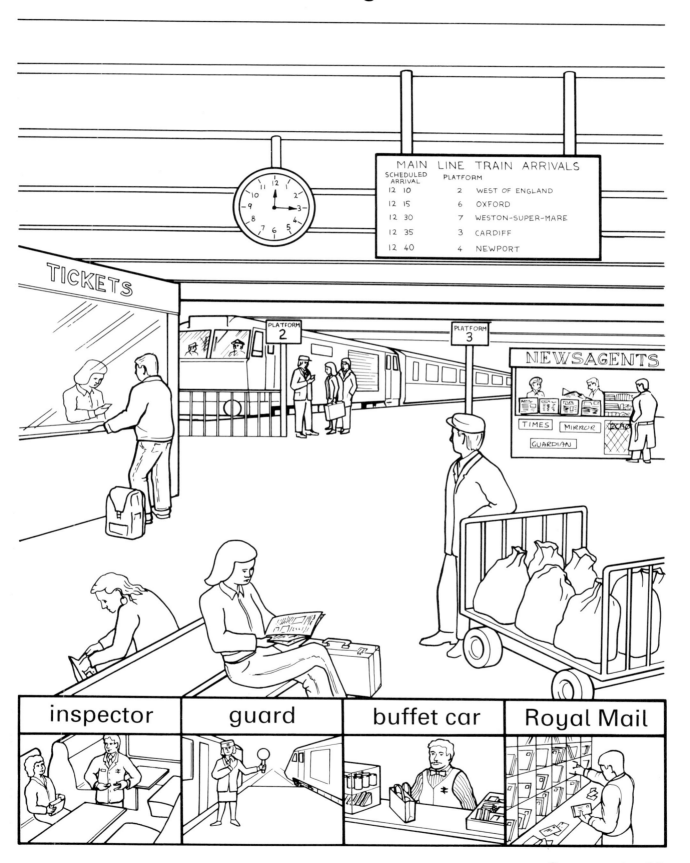

MAIN LINE TRAIN ARRIVALS

SCHEDULED ARRIVAL	PLATFORM	
12 10	2	WEST OF ENGLAND
12 15	6	OXFORD
12 30	7	WESTON-SUPER-MARE
12 35	3	CARDIFF
12 40	4	NEWPORT

TICKETS

PLATFORM 2

PLATFORM 3

NEWSAGENTS

TIMES   MIRROR   ?
GUARDIAN

inspector	guard	buffet car	Royal Mail

Transport

car	bus	van
tanker	milk float	motor bike
coach	lorry	helicopter
Underground train	aeroplane	bike

Where we find water

waterfall	lake
sea	stream
canal	reservoir
pond	river

Journey to the sea

source	stream	waterfall	river	sea

Water comes and goes

When the sun shines, water **evaporates** into the air.

Water in clouds falls as rain or snow.

Pond creatures

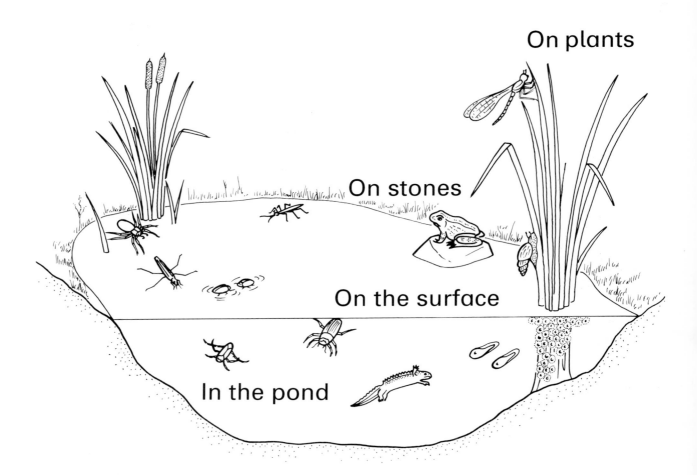

pond snail	water measurer	whirligig beetle	great diving beetle	tadpoles	frog spawn
pond skater	newt	water boatman	frog	spider	dragonfly

Water plants

By the sea

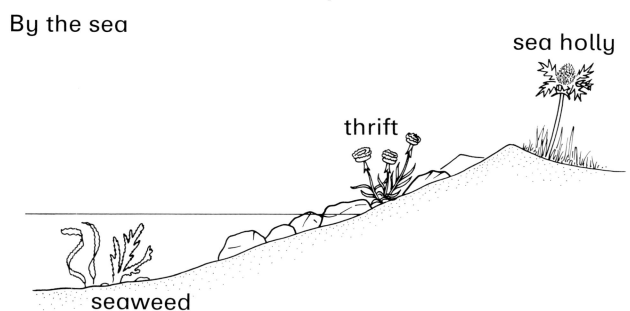

sea holly

thrift

seaweed

In fresh water

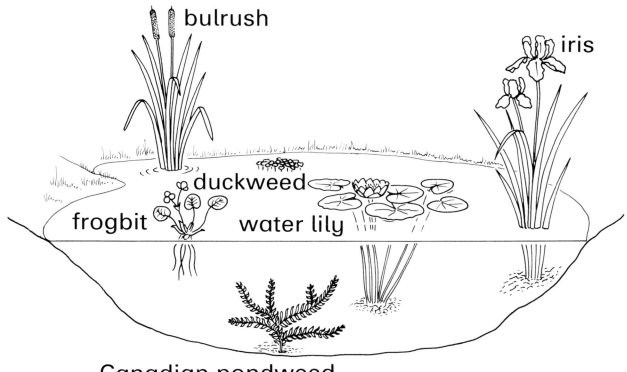

bulrush

iris

duckweed

frogbit

water lily

Canadian pondweed

Water birds

In lakes and rivers

mute swan

heron

tufted duck

drake mallard

ducklings

mallard duck

Canada goose

A duck

large bill for scooping
water and food

strong feathers for flying

oil gland

webbed feet for paddling

Copymaster 87

Water transport

hovercraft

ferry

tug

cargo ship

barge

pleasure boat

Fun on the water

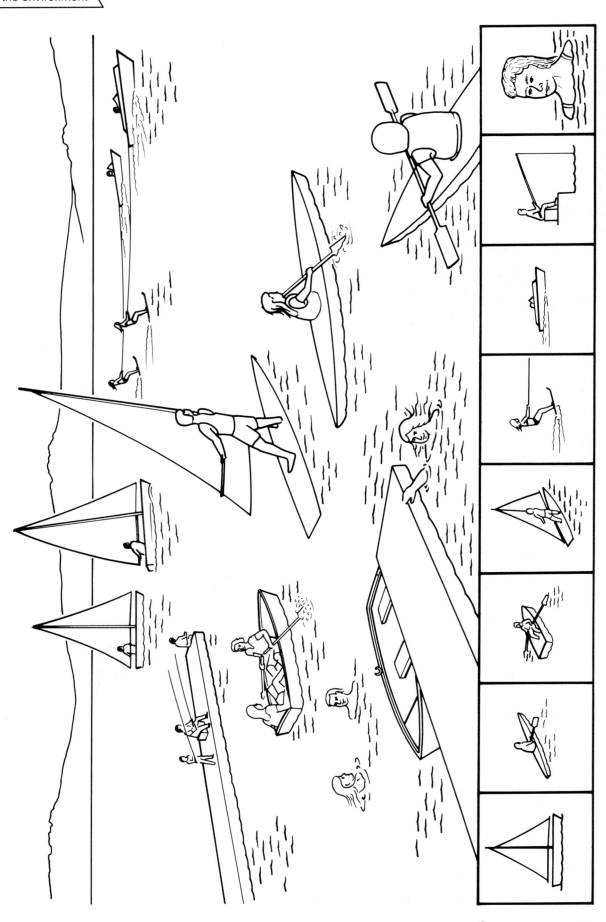

Using water

Make a weather record

sun	rain	cloud	snow	cloud/sun

Monday	Tuesday	Wed	Thursday	Friday

Day	Weather	Temp. °C	
Monday			
Tuesday			
Wednesday			
Thursday			
Friday			

The weather chart

Spring

March
April
May

Summer

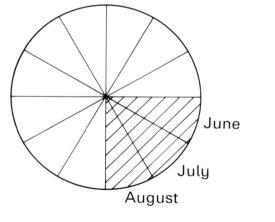

June

July

August

Autumn

November

October

September

Winter

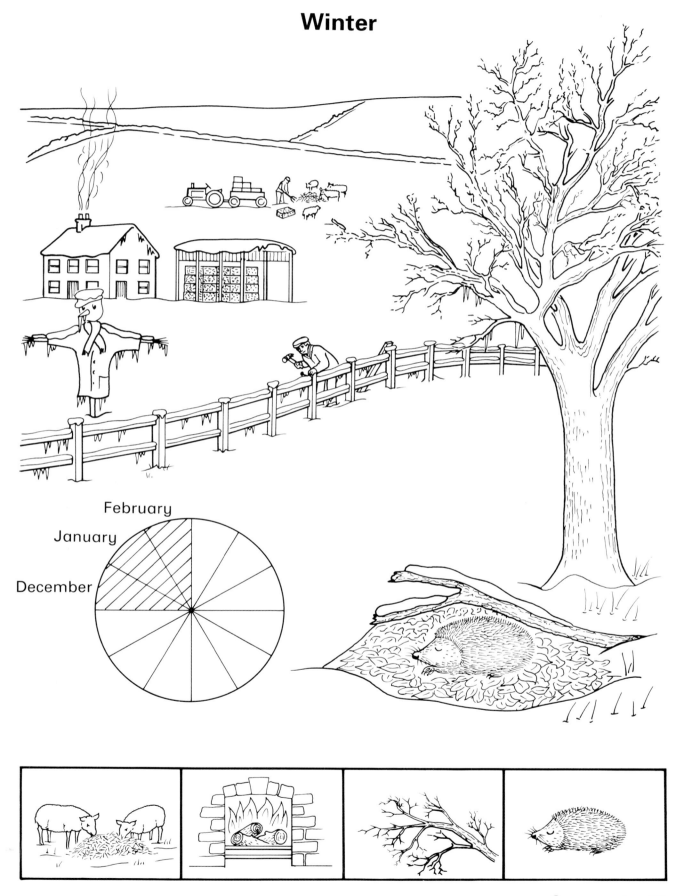

Living in the Arctic

arctic weather

Jan Feb March April May June July Aug Sept Oct Nov Dec

freezing

cold   cold

cool

wooden houses are warm to live in

transport by husky team or snow mobile

Arctic plants and animals

lichens	moss	saxifrage

walrus	seal

caribou deer	polar bear

Living in a desert

desert weather

Jan · Feb · March · April · May · June · July · Aug · Sept · Oct · Nov · Dec

hot and dry

very hot and dry

houses

transport

Desert plants and animals

cactus	oasis palms
lizard	camel

Living in a rainforest

rainforest weather

Jan Feb March April May June July Aug Sept Oct Nov Dec

very hot and wet

houses

transport

Rainforest plants and animals

| parrot | trees, creepers and flowers |

1 Green
2 Brown
3 Red
4 Grey
5 Cream

| tree-frog | monkey |

Mountains

Hills

farm	spring	fields		
stream	village	wood	footpath	hill

The coast

cliffs	rock pools	sea	beach	sand dune	groyne

The countryside

FOOTPATH

farm	wood	village	hedge	field	stile

Copymaster 106

Marshes

| | | | | reed bed |
| --- | --- | --- | --- | river |